Christianity
and the Poor

Quinton Howitt

Quinton Howitt Publications
Email: quinton@vineyardbi.org

Copyright © Quinton Howitt 2011

First published on Kindle 2012

Published in paperpack 2014

The Scripture quotations in this publication are taken from:
  The Darby Bible (DBY)
  The English Standard Version (ESV)
  The King James Version (KJV)
  The New American Standard Bible (1977) (NAS)
  The New American Standard Bible (1995) (NAU)
  The New International Version (1984-US) (NIV)
  The New Jerusalem Bible (NJB)
  The New King James Version (NKJV)
  The New Living Translation (NLT)
  The New Revised Standard Version (NRSV)
  The Revised Standard Version (RSV)
  The Revised Webster Update (RWB)
  Young's Literal Translation (YLT)

ISBN 13: 978-1500488420
ISBN 10: 1500488429

Contents

Introduction

"Some 22,000 children under 5 ... die each day, with some 70% of these deaths occurring in the first year of the child's life."[1] It has been estimated that over the past 50 years, 400 million people have died as a result of hunger and poor sanitation. To put this figure into perspective, that is three times the number of people killed in all wars fought in the entire 20th century.[2]

These are staggering statistics, so shocking in fact, that 1) we tend to forget we are talking about living, breathing human beings here and 2) we, as individuals or local churches, feel defeated before we have really even begun to look for ways to alleviate and/or overcome the problems.

I must admit that I had to wrestle with a similar defeatist attitude when I began writing this book. How could I possibly achieve anything beneficial by writing a book about a problem of this magnitude? After all, there has already been much written about poverty alleviation. I was then reminded that the Lord works in ways we cannot understand. He has a way of accomplishing mighty things through small beginnings, and while there is a lot of material out there on

[1]Unicef: Child Mortality Rates http://www.unicefusa.org/news/releases/child-mortality-rate-drops.html
[2]Global Hunger Fact Sheet, "World Food Programme Facts and Figures," Italy, Rome: *World Food Programme,* 2003, p. 1.

the subject, there is actually very little biblical and practical theology examination of it. This then brings me to the purpose of this book.

This book will provide you, and hopefully through you, your local church, an awareness of some of the facts concerning the dire position of the poor worldwide. It will also equip you with a "substantial" biblical knowledge of poor, God's concern for them, and His expectations for you and I in regard to them. Lastly, it will serve as an eye-opener to the current ways in which local churches typically assist the poor; this should stimulate thought towards additional and more effective methods of attacking the problem.

It is my prayer and hope that having worked through the contents of this book, you will be dynamically challenged and motivated to both teach about and do the work of caring for the poor.

The approach I will follow in this book will be as follows. In Section A, I will paint a picture of the reality we face in regards to the poor in the 21ˢᵗ century. I will then endeavour to define and explain poverty and its measurement, since we cannot address the problem effectively until we have a good grasp of what we are dealing with. Following this, in Section B, I will turn to the scriptures and provide a detailed analysis of the biblical language of social justice. Chapters in this section of the book will include:

1. An outline of the biblical terminology for the poor.
2. Considering them as a sociological group.
3. Special classes of the poor.
4. General evidence of concern for them.
5. God's concern for special classes of the poor.
6. God's response to them, and finally,
7. The Christian's response to the poor.

In Section C, I will finish by highlighting and commenting on various methods local churches utilize in their attempts to minister to the poor.

SECTION A

Poverty and the Poor

The Reality We Face

World hunger estimates are very bleak indeed. During the period 2006-2009, world under nourishment[3] levels reached an all-time high with 1,023 billion suffering this fate.[4] This was partly due to exorbitant food prices and a global economic crisis. Since then, the number of undernourished persons has decreased somewhat to 925 million (see figure 1).

Broken down, developing countries account for 98 percent of the world's undernourished people and have a prevalence of under nourishment of 16 percent (Figure 2).[5]

The problem though is that despite the drop, the number of undernourished people in the world is staggering. It is higher than it has ever been apart from the period listed above. Of huge

---

[3]"Under nourishment exists when caloric intake is below the minimum dietary energy requirement (MDER). The MDER is the amount of energy needed for light activity and to maintain a minimum acceptable weight for attained height. It varies by country and from year to year depending on the gender and age structure of the population. Throughout this report, the words 'hunger' and 'under nourishment' are used interchangeably." "Arslan, A. The State of Food Insecurity in the World. Monitoring progress towards the World Food Summit and Millennium Development Goals" (Rome, Italy), report of the Food and Agricultural Organization of the United Nations, 2010, p. 8.
[4]Ibid.
[5]Ibid.

concern to many is what will take place if another or even more serious economic crisis arises?

Figure 1

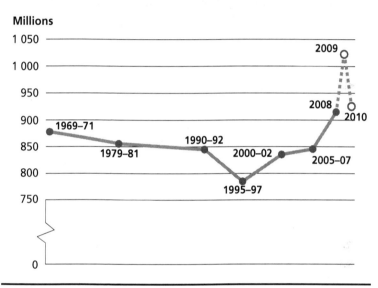

Note: Figures for 2009 and 2010 are estimated by FAO with input from the United States Department of Agriculture, Economic Research Service.

Source: FAO.

This is a very real scenario at present considering the European debt crisis and mind boggling US debt figures (upwards of $14 trillion). In this past economic crisis, it was evident that the poorer countries are vulnerable to economic shocks. They simply do not have the mechanisms in place to protect the poor.[6]

---

[6]Ibid.

Figure 2

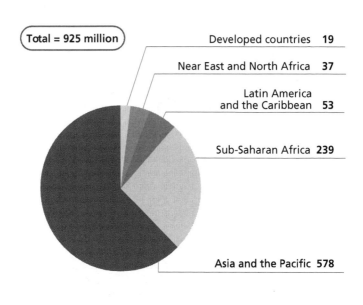

Undernourishment in 2010, by region (millions)

Total = 925 million

Developed countries **19**

Near East and North Africa **37**

Latin America
and the Caribbean **53**

Sub-Saharan Africa **239**

Asia and the Pacific **578**

Note: All figures are rounded.   *Source:* FAO.

At a regional level, it is evident that levels of under nourishment have been reduced in Asia and Sub-Saharan Africa. In contrast with this though, levels in Latin America, the Caribbean, Near East and North Africa are still increasing to some extent[7] (see figure 3).

---

[7]Ibid., p. 11.

Figure 3

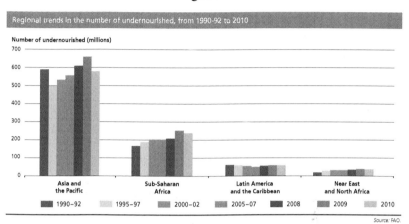

Regional trends in the number of undernourished, from 1990-92 to 2010

Number of undernourished (millions)

1990–92 1995–97 2000–02 2005–07 2008 2009 2010

Source: FAO.

The proportion of undernourished people is highest in sub-Saharan Africa at approximately 30 percent in 2010 (Figure 4), but progress varies widely at the country level.

"As of 2005–07 (the most recent period for which complete data is available), the Congo, Ghana, Mali and Nigeria had already achieved MDG 1[8] and Ethiopia and others were close to achieving it; in the Democratic Republic of the Congo, however, the proportion of under nourishment had risen to 69 percent (from 26 percent in 1990–92). In Asia, Armenia, Myanmar and Vietnam had achieved MDG 1 and China and others were close to doing so, while in Latin America and the Caribbean, Guyana, Jamaica and Nicaragua had achieved MDG 1 and Brazil, and others were approaching the target reduction."[9]

---

[8]Millennium Development Goal.

[9]"The State of Food Insecurity in the World. Monitoring progress towards the World Food Summit and Millennium Development Goals" (Rome, Italy), report of the Food and Agricultural Organization of the United Nations, 2010, p. 11.

Figure 4

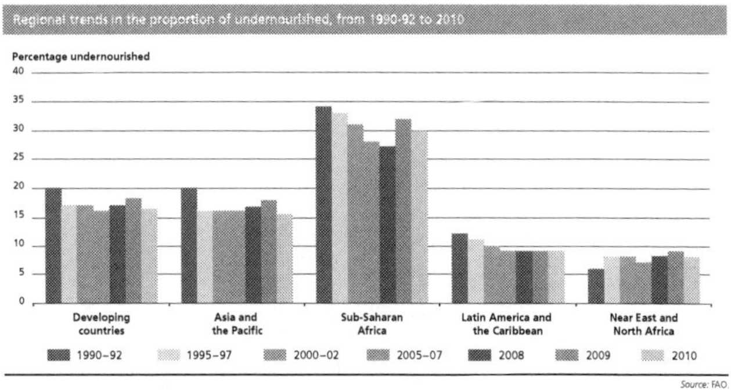

World Hunger Hotspots

According to the FAO, as of 2006, 40 countries faced serious food shortages requiring international aid,[10] which is up from 36 in 2003.[11] As figure 5[12] indicates, most of those countries fall within the continent of Africa, and more specifically, Sub-Saharan Africa. At present, "Sub-Saharan Africa is officially the poorest region in the world."[13]

---

[10]FOA Newsroom. 40 Countries face food shortages worldwide. Available [Online] at http://www.fao.org/newsroom/en/news/2006/1000416/index.html

[11]"The State of Food Insecurity in the World. Monitoring progress towards the World Food Summit and Millennium Development Goals" (Rome, Italy), report of the Food and Agricultural Organization of the United Nations, 2010, p. 14.

[12]Fighting Hunger Worldwide. Available [Online] at: http://documents.wfp.org/stellent/groups/public/documents/communications/wfp229327.pdf

All of the countries appearing on the map have experienced severe food shortages for at least two consecutive years and many for as long as ten years.

[13]G. Mills. *Poverty to Prosperity. Globalisation, Good Governance and African*

To the north, conditions are far worse, what with pre-famine conditions being reported in Eritrea and various regions of Ethiopia. In these areas there has been massive crop failure, and the livestock are dying as a result of a shortage of water and food. Millions of people need emergency food aid.[14]

Recovery, Johannesburg: The South African Institute of International Affairs and Tafelberg, 2002, p. 86. This statistic is still applicable in 2011.
[14]Ibid.

Figure 5

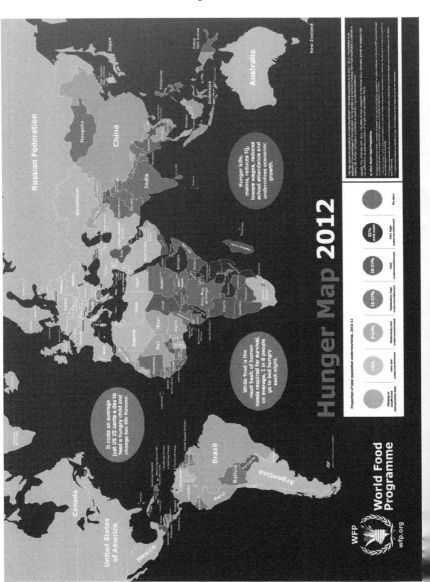

The Depth of Hunger

The number of people suffering from hunger is not the only cause for concern for hunger alleviation pundits. According to the FAO, effectively fighting hunger requires knowledge of both the number of people and the depth of hunger sufferance.[15] A food deficit measurement was established in the report "The State of Food Insecurity in the World 2000."[16] This measurement serves as an indicator of how severely the dietary energy intake of undernourished people falls short of their minimum needs.[17]

Using this measurement, it has been estimated that the bulk of the 925 million people who suffer from chronic hunger lack between 90 and 430 kilocalories per day.[18] It is important to note however that a large proportion of these people do not appear emaciated, but only thin. The problem is that it creates the

---

[15]The depth of hunger sufferance is reflected in the amount of kilocalories missing from the diets of undernourished people. The greater the deficit of kilocalories, the great the vulnerability to nutrition related health risks. It is common knowledge that frail, unhealthy people cannot fulfil their potential. A nation of frail, unhealthy people cannot progress. "The State of Food Insecurity in the World. When people live with hunger and fear of starvation." (Rome, Italy), report of the Food and Agricultural Organization of the United Nations, 2000, p. 1.

[16]*Food insecurity* exists when people do not have adequate physical, social or economic access to food as defined above. "The State of Food Insecurity in the World. When people live with hunger and fear of starvation." (Rome, Italy), report of the Food and Agricultural Organization of the United Nations, 2010, p. 8.

[17]This measurement compares the average amount of dietary energy that undernourished people get from the food they eat with the minimum amount of dietary energy they need to maintain body weight and undertake light activity.

[18]On average, a person needs about 1800 kcal per day as a minimum energy intake. Refer to the Worldbank report for detailed statistics reflecting the depth of hunger experienced in various countries. Available [Online] at: http://data.worldbank.org/indicator/SN.ITK.DPTH

illusion that people are not really suffering when, in fact, they are; the human body has defence mechanisms which compensate for lack of food by slowing down physical activity, or in the case of children, growth. Chronic hunger means a number of things:

- That people, and particularly children, are highly susceptible to disease,
- That children may be languid and incapable of concentrating in school,
- That mothers may give birth to underweight babies, and adults may lack the energy to fulfil their potential.[19]

Statistics reveal that while there might be a greater number of people suffering from hunger in Asia and the Pacific, the depths of hunger are clearly the most prevalent in Sub-Saharan Africa. It is estimated that the proportion of undernourished people remains at 30 percent in 2010 (see figure 4)[20].

Hidden Hunger

Probably the biggest cause for alarm is that presented by "Hidden Hunger."[21] Micronutrients[22] are the fundamental building blocks for human growth, development and proper functioning.[23] When

---

[19]"The State of Food Insecurity in the World. When people live with hunger and fear of starvation," (Rome, Italy), report of the Food and Agricultural Organization of the United Nations, 2000, p. 1.

[20]"The State of Food Insecurity in the World. Monitoring progress towards the World Food Summit and Millennium Development Goals" (Rome, Italy), report of the Food and Agricultural Organization of the United Nations, 2010, p. 11.

[21]"Hidden Hunger" is the term used to describe micronutrient deficiency.

[22]Vitamins and minerals.

[23]P. Shetty. "The State of Food Insecurity in the World. When people must live with hunger and fear starvation" (Italy, Rome), report of the Food and Agricultural Organization of the United Nations, 2002, p.24.

they are deficient, severe chronic problems arise.

The degree of micronutrient deficiencies is fairly common knowledge; anaemia impacts about 2 billion people in the world. That is approximately one-third of the world population, women suffering the most. Most of the 2 billion can be found residing in developing countries[24] (see figure 6 below).[25]

Figure 6

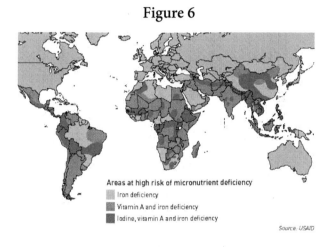

Areas at high risk of micronutrient deficiency

    Iron deficiency

    Vitamin A and iron deficiency

    Iodine, vitamin A and iron deficiency

Source: USAID

Those most commonly affected by micronutrient deficiency are women and children, mainly because children require large amounts of micronutrients to sustain normal growth patterns and women, on average, require higher levels of iron, particularly during pregnancy.[26]

"Five micronutrients stand apart, both because of their importance

---

[24]The Micronutrient Report. Current progress and trends in the control of vitamin A, iodine, and iron deficiencies (Canada, Ottawa), report of the Micronutrient Initiative, 2001, p. 1.
[25]"Economic Rationale for Investing in Micronutrient Programs, A Policy Brief Based on New Analyses," Washington, DC, *USAID*, 1992.
[26]Ibid.

and the numbers of people who are deficient in them. These micronutrients have become the focus of highly successful programs that have reached millions of children and adults. [Table 1] shows just how much difference they make."[27] Of course, reading into this table, one can also see the devastating impact micronutrient depravation has upon children who are not exposed to the programs.

Table 1

MICRONUTRIENT	IMPACT THROUGH PROGRAMMES
VITAMIN A	• 23% reduction in under-five mortality rates • 70% reduction in childhood blindness
IODINE	• 13-point increase in IQ
IRON	• 20% reduction in maternal mortality
ZINC	• 6% reduction in child mortality • 27% reduction in diarrhoea incidence in children
FOLATE	• 50% reduction in severe neural tube birth defects, such as Spina Bifida

---

[27]"Investing in the future: A United Call to Action on Vitamin and Mineral Deficiencies." *Global Report.* 2009, pp. 4-5.

Table 2

TYPE OF REPERCUSSION	NUMBERS AFFECTED
LIVES LOST ANNUALLY	• 1.1 million children under five die due to vitamin A and zinc deficiencies • 136,000 woman and children die because of iron deficiency anaemia
LIVES IMPAIRED ANNUALLY	• 18 million babies are born mentally impaired because of maternal iodine deficiency • 150,000 babies are born with severe birth defects due to inadequate maternal foliate intake • 350,000 children become blind due to vitamin A deficiency
LOST PRODUCTIVITY	• 1.6 billion people suffer reduced productive capacity due to anaemia

Table 2[28] is a further illustration of the significant repercussions of vitamin deficiency.

In practice, vitamin and mineral deficiencies (VMD) overlap and interact. Half of the children with VMD are suffering from multiple deficiencies, adding up an immeasurable burden on individuals, on health services and education systems.

An Analysis of the Causes of the Problems

When looking at the problem, one must keep in mind its differing dimensions. There is a clear lack of food and hundreds of millions of people are lacking key micronutrients, which jeopardize their quality of life.

It has become apparent that no definitive answers can be given as to why so many people are suffering from food shortage. The suggestions range from genocide,[29] warfare and civil unrest,[30]

---

[28]Ibid., p. 7.

[29]Rwanda in 1994.

[30]An example of this being the Ivory Coast, which is now a nation rent by

disease,[31] climate abnormalities,[32] corruption,[33] abuse of food aid schemes by dictators and dishonest government officials,[34] and the rejection of genetically modified foods (GM Foods).[35] However, according to Jacques Diouf (FAO Director General), careful investigation does single out numerous aspects that distinguish the successful countries from those that incurred a set back. He goes on to suggest that countries who have been effective in reducing hunger were marked by economic growth, lower levels of HIV infection and specifically, more rapid growth in their agricultural sectors.[36] The findings pertaining to "growth in the agricultural sector" are in agreement with the analysis conducted by the World Food Summit (WFS) Plan of Action, which emphasized the significance of growth in the agricultural sector to ensure food security.[37] It is safe to say that one of the more significant causes of

---

political turmoil. Available [Online] at:
http://seattlepi.nwsource.com/africa/ivory22.shtml

[31]HIV/AIDS, Malaria, Hepatitis, Cholera, Tuberculosis, and Haemorrhagic fevers.

[32]See Appendix 1.

[33]"Corruption is one of the major factors holding back Africa's economic growth", Ex South African Finance Minister Trevor Manuel, *Finance 24,* 2004.

[34]President of Zimbabwe, Robert Mugabe, and his political party, the Zanu PF can be cited as an example of this.

[35]GM Food AID, *Lusaka Declaration.* According to numerous countries in Africa, some of which include Zambia, Mozambique, South Africa, and Ethiopia have serious concerns about the use of GM foods and would prefer not to use them. Articles demonstrating opposition to GM foods are available [Online] at:
http://www.connectotel.com/gmfood/gmafrica.html

[36]"The State of Food Insecurity in the World. Monitoring progress towards the World Food Summit and Millennium Development Goals" (Rome, Italy), report of the Food and Agricultural Organization of the United Nations, 2003, p. 4.

[37]The WFS plan of action has undertaken to encourage, where appropriate,

food insecurity is a lack of proper agricultural infrastructure and practice.

Agriculture and agricultural trade play a vital role in developing countries' national economy and food security. Statistics reveal that in the developing world, agriculture accounts for a significant percentage of Gross Domestic Product (GDP) and more than half of total employment. What is even more noteworthy is that in countries where there is serious food shortage, these figures grow considerably.[38]

It has been proven that economic growth founded in agriculture can have a significant impact in poverty and hunger reduction. By increasing employment and incomes in agriculture, demand for non-agricultural goods and services are encouraged, allowing for an improvement on non-farm rural incomes as well.[39]

We turn now to the latter dimension: lack of sufficient micronutrients. Micronutrient malnutrition occurs when a person's diet offers them insufficient amounts of vitamins and minerals. Those vitamins and minerals usually lacking the most are folate, iodine, iron, selenium, vitamin A and C.

According to the FAO, in the neediest of regions, it has been

---

the production and use of culturally appropriate, traditional and underutilized food crops, including grains, oilseeds, pulses, root crops, fruits and vegetables, promoting home and, where appropriate, school gardens and urban agriculture, using sustainable technologies, and encourage the sustainable utilization of unused or underutilized fish resources. "Rome Declaration of World Food Security," *The World Food Summit,* held from the 13th -17th November 1996 in Rome, Italy. Available[Online] at: http://www.fao.org/docrep/003/w3613e/w3613e00.htm

[38]"The State of Food Insecurity in the World. Monitoring progress towards the World Food Summit and Millennium Development Goals" (Rome, Italy), report of the Food and Agricultural Organization of the United Nations, 2003, p. 16.

[39]Ibid.

found that many people's diets are totally deficient, of the starchy staple foods (carbohydrate - rich maize, potatoes, rice, wheat and cassava) that provide energy. However, in regions suffering from moderate food insecurity, people typically receive enough of the staple starchy foods. The critical problem here is they lack a variety of other foods that make up a nutritious diet: legumes, meat, fish, oils, dairy products, vegetables and fruit, which provide protein, fat and micronutrients as well as energy.[40] Providing them with a well-balanced diet is essential to "household food security."[41]

The three key approaches to minimising micronutrient deficiency are dietary diversity, food fortification and supplementation.[42] Most micronutrient deficiencies could be eliminated by modifying diets to include a greater diversity of nutrient-rich foods. *This could be achieved by* promoting home vegetable gardens, community fish ponds, and livestock[43] (My emphasis).

The suggestion of promoting home vegetable gardens has been successfully demonstrated by the Medical Research Council of South Africa in a rural village in KwaZulu/Natal. Diets of the children in the village were found to consist mainly of porridge, bread and rice, hence lacking key vitamin A micronutrients. The programme altered this by encouraging the cultivation of vegetables,

---

[40]P. Shetty. "The State of Food Insecurity in the World. When people must live with hunger and fear starvation" (Italy, Rome), report of the Food and Agricultural Organization of the United Nations, 2002, p.24.

[41]"Household food security" can be defined as access by all households at all times to adequate safe and nutritious food for a healthy and productive life. S. Bont-Ankomah. "Addressing food insecurity in South Africa." Paper presented at the SARPN conference on Land Reform and Poverty Alleviation in Southern Africa Pretoria. June 2001, p. 2.

[42]P. Shetty. "The State of Food Insecurity in the World. When people must live with hunger and fear starvation' (Italy, Rome), report of the Food and Agricultural Organization of the United Nations, 2002, p.24.

[43]Ibid.

such as carrots, pumpkins and spinach, which are rich in beta-carotene and by educating villagers to include them in their daily food intake. The results were astonishing. One year into the programme, children were found to have measurable improvements in vitamin-A status, which is primarily responsible for boosting the immune system.[44]

Thus, having analysed the dimensions of the problem, it appears as if the solution may well lie in an agricultural approach.

Drought and HIV/AIDS

Before moving on, this section would be incomplete without mentioning the impact of drought and HIV/AIDS.

Drought

There is a close tie between food security and water. If a solution to food insecurity lies in an agricultural approach, then one definite stumbling block is a lack of water availability. Something has to be done to ensure adequate water. Agriculture is the largest user of water consuming approximately 69 percent of all withdrawals worldwide and more than 80 percent in developing countries.[45] Access to abundant water ensures agricultural yield increases and lowers the levels of under nourishment.

To illustrate the vital role water plays, Drought was listed as a major cause of food emergencies. "Africa is both the driest

---

[44]Faber, M., Jogessar, V.B. & Benadé, A.J.S. 2001. "Nutritional status and dietary intakes of children aged 2-5 years and their caregivers in a rural South African community," *International Journal of Food Sciences and Nutrition*, 52(5): pp. 401-411.

[45]"The State of Food Insecurity in the World. Monitoring progress towards the World Food Summit and Millennium Development Goals" (Rome, Italy), report of the Food and Agricultural Organization of the United Nations, 2003, p. 12.

continent other than Oceania and the region where hunger is most prevalent."[46]

HIV/AIDS

Turning to the HIV/AIDS crisis; a global summary of the HIV/AIDS epidemic revealed certain alarming statistics:[47]

The impact of AIDS on food insecurity was first emphasized in 2002-2003 when more than fourteen million people in Southern Africa faced a food crisis. The FAO demonstrated that hunger cannot be combated effectively in regions ravaged by AIDS, unless interventions address the particular needs of AIDS-affected households and incorporate measures both to prevent and to mitigate the spread of HIV/AIDS.[48] I stated previously that Sub-Saharan people suffer the most from under nourishment and

---

46Ibid. "The current drought in Somalia is…the worst the country has seen in 36 years. Most areas have received little or no rain for nine months. Pasture is depleted and cattle and goats are dying in large numbers, leaving thousands of animal carcasses littering the roadsides. People are seeing riverbeds dry for the first time in their lives. Families are becoming destitute. They are dependent on livestock for survival, and have resorted to desperate measures to try to keep their animals alive. Many have used food normally kept for the family to feed their dying herds, some even going so far as to take the grass off the roofs of their houses, leaving them without adequate shelter. Children in particular are suffering from a lack of food and water. In some areas, malnutrition is affecting over 30% of children, one of the highest rates in the world." *Drought crisis leaves struggling Somalia on the brink* (2011). Sarah Robinson, Concern Worldwide program advisor for Somalia. Guardian. Available [Online] at:
http://www.guardian.co.uk/global-development/poverty-matters/2011/jun/06/somalia-devastated-by-drought-crisis
47See Appendix 2.
48"The State of Food Insecurity in the World. Monitoring progress towards the World Food Summit and Millennium Development Goals" (Rome, Italy), report of the Food and Agricultural Organization of the United Nations, 2003, p. 12.

depth of hunger. This correlates with this region also having by far the highest number of adults and children living with HIV; more than 67.5% of the total 33.3 million people living with HIV worldwide reside there.

Reports suggest that the Southern African crisis was caused by a combination of droughts, failed economic policies and civil strife. However, it was severely compounded by the AIDS epidemic which had broken up millions of families, destabilized the food sector and weakened the capacity of governments to respond.[49]

Although governments and food relief organizations came to the rescue, reports suggested that a new type of emergency was looming on the horizon, that being severe short term food shortages were coinciding with unmatched collapses in health, agricultural production and food security. What makes matters worse is that these problems are set to continue for decades.

There is a negative and positive relationship that exists between HIV/AIDS and the agriculture sector. The negative relationship is that AIDS severely affects food security in the following ways:

Many of those who die from the AIDS epidemic are young adults in the prime of their working careers. When they die they create an imbalance in the population leaving behind the elderly and the young. This trend seriously influences agricultural farm production levels and hence food security. It has been suggested that by 2020, AIDS will have killed one-fifth of the agricultural labour force in many southern African countries. In hard-hit areas, research has shown that more than half of all households are headed by women (30 percent mostly widows), grandparents (20 percent)

---

[49]"The State of Food Insecurity in the World. Monitoring progress towards the World Food Summit and Millennium Development Goals" (Rome, Italy), report of the Food and Agricultural Organization of the United Nations, 2003, p. 11.

and orphaned children (5 percent)[50] (see figure 7). This has caused a catastrophic shortage in labour, resources and knowledge of how to grow staple and commercial crops, which has further resulted in families either discarding their fields or only growing survival crops. One research project revealed that maize production in Zimbabwean communal agriculture had dropped by 61 percent in households that suffered from AIDS-related deaths[51] (see figure 8[52]).

Figure 7   **Figure 8**

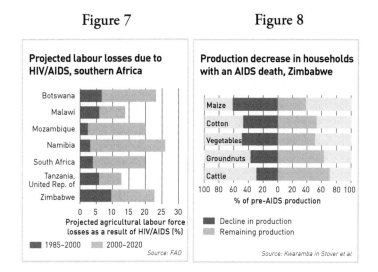

[50]Ibid.

[51]Ibid.

[52]J. Stover, L. Bollinger, R Kerkhoven, G Mutangadura, D & Mukurazita. *The economic impact of AIDS in Zimbabwe,* Washington: The Futures Group International, 1999, p. 15.

AIDS lessens investment in agriculture. Money that would have been utilized to purchase food, seeds and seedlings is used instead to pay off medical bills and funeral expenses. Young children, mostly girls, are required to leave school and either work or look after ill parents. This prevents the cross-pollination of essential knowledge and skills between generations. "In two districts in Kenya affected by AIDS, a study found that only 7 percent of orphans heading farm households had adequate agricultural knowledge."[53]

The positive relationship between the agricultural sector and HIV/AIDS is that "the onset and progression of the disease is delayed in well-nourished HIV-infected people."

This concludes the first chapter and as I said in the introduction, the objective has been to give you a cursory idea of the facts concerning the dire position of the poor worldwide. If you would like to gain a far deeper and more specific picture of what we face, I suggest that you review some of the materials I have utilized to write this chapter. These materials are listed in the footnotes and bibliography.

---

[53]"The State of Food Insecurity in the World. Monitoring progress towards the World Food Summit and Millennium Development Goals" (Rome, Italy), report of the Food and Agricultural Organization of the United Nations, 2003, p. 6.

Approaches to Poverty

Starvation, clearly, is the most telling aspect of poverty.

Nobel Prize winner, Amartya Sen.[54]

The manifestation of poverty has begun to receive more attention, and its eradication is becoming an important concern of those interested in the developing countries. Evidence of this can be seen in that the Millennium Goals, agreed by the 149 countries at the United Nations Millennium Summit in New York, aimed to reduce poverty by half by 2015. Furthermore, the World Bank and other major donors are now assessing their social policies in light of whether they impact upon poverty.

The irony, however, is that although there is tremendous emphasis and support for the eradication of poverty, there appears to be a lack of clarity as to exactly what poverty is or means. This poses a problem because, in order to devise strategies for poverty reduction, *one must first have a clear understanding of what it is you are trying to correct.*

Furthermore, the current approaches to the identification of poverty and to policy formulation are muddled: on the one hand there is recognition of its multidimensionality; while on the other

---

[54]A. Sen. *Poverty and Famines: An Essay on Entitlement and Deprivation.* (New York: Oxford Press, 1981), pp. 11-12.

hand, the income approach continues to enjoy dominance in determining descriptions and analysis.[55] Just how poverty is defined is vitally important when one considers that different definitions of poverty imply use of different criteria for measurement, the identification of different individuals and groups as poor, and the use of different policy solutions for poverty reduction.[56]

In this chapter, I will briefly outline various definitions and methods of measuring poverty. As you read through this chapter, try to identify important details that could help you to build a clearer picture of what it is, so that you can begin crystallizing in your mind how you might better serve the poor in your community.

Difficulties in Defining and Measuring Poverty

Why is poverty so difficult to define? Laderchi, Saith and Stewart[57] note some of the difficulties encountered when trying to define and measure poverty.

- First, it is difficult to know in which "space" to define and measure poverty or deprivation. Should it be defined and measured under *resources* or *utilities* (what people have and do not have), *capabilities* (the ability of people to reach their potential and achieve), or *functionings* (what people are actually doing or being). Second, there is the "sphere of concerns" which questions whether the definition should be material, social, cultural, political or all of the above. In the latter case,

---

[55]C. Laderchi, R. Saith, F. Stewart. "Everyone agrees we need poverty reduction, but not what this means: does this matter?" (Paper for Wider Conference on Inequality, Poverty and Human Well being. Helsinki, 30-31 May 2003.), p. 3.
[56]Ibid.
[57]Ibid.

this would make defining poverty extremely complex.

- Another aspect complicating matters is *universality*. Must the definition be applicable to different societies or to one type of society, i.e. should it be of the type that is easily transposed over any and all countries? At present it appears as if approaches to poverty are society specific; that is that they are best designed to extract certain characteristics from a society to the detriment of others. For instance, the "income based" approach to poverty was devised for measuring poverty in developed countries whereas the "capabilities" approach was devised for developing countries.

- There is the question of trying to establish a definition and measurement of poverty which is *objective*. Most statements about poverty point to some sort of objectivity: i.e. there is some reality out there which poverty statistics measure. The problem is that, as yet, no poverty definitions exist in the absence of some sort of value judgement, and where there is a value judgement, there cannot be total objectivity.

Another difficulty regards the *time* period over which poverty should be measured, i.e. a month, a year or longer. The length of time defined in the specific poverty approach can distort true poverty figures. One challenge comes when one is met with the realization that many people move in and out of poverty on a regular basis. If one is measuring poverty over a short period of time, there is the danger that the "transitory poor" will be missed out, i.e. they might be in the middle of an upward phase and hence above poverty lines. On the other hand however, longer measurements of poverty tend to only reflect the "chronic poor", or at the very least lessen the devastation of the "transitory poor", i.e. the measurement reflects an average poverty figure and does not reveal the true depth of poverty.

- Another important issue which poses difficulty regards the determination of *poverty lines*. Two concerns emerge here. First, there is debate as to whether the poverty line, which separates those in poverty from those who are not, should be defined relative to the average achievements in a society (relative poverty[58]) or should it rather reflect some absolute standards of deprivation (absolute poverty[59]). Second, there is the question of where the poverty line should be drawn. For instance, when trying to define relative poverty lines, the problem arises in that there is no technical justification for any specific line; it is usually determined subjectively through a political decision based on some statistical facts. In the case of absolute poverty, determining a dividing line rests upon whether there is some sort of discontinuity between the poor and the non-poor which can be evidenced in the poverty line. It can be a complex process trying to find these discontinuities.

- The issue of the *unit* over which poverty is defined also poses a number of complexities; units may include the individual, the household or geographics. Current definitions allow for measurements of one or another unit, to the disadvantage of the

---

[58]"Relative poverty" is a *poverty* measure based on a poor *standard of living* or a low *income* relative to the rest of society. Unlike *absolute poverty*, it does not necessarily imply that physical human necessities *of nutrition, health and shelter* cannot be met; instead it suggests that the lack of access to many of the goods and services expected by the rest of the contemporary *society* leads to social exclusion and damaging results for the individuals and families in relative poverty. World History.Com. Relative Poverty in the News.

[59]"Absolute poverty" is defined as "a condition characterised by severe deprivation of basic human needs, including food, safe drinking water, sanitation facilities, health, shelter, education and information. It depends not only on income but also on access to services." D. Gordon. "Definitions of Concepts for the Perceptions of Poverty and Social Exclusion." Available [Online] at: http://www.bris.ac.uk/poverty/pse/99-Pilot/99-Pilot_1.pdf

others. For instance, it is usually the individuals who are suffering, yet, in the case of the income based definitions; scientists only measure household and some resource data (money income, sanitation, and clean water). The problem is that it is difficult to know how these amenities are distributed throughout the household. In the case of geographical units of measure, scientists typically focus on either identifying the society against which the poverty lines are drawn, or they define the boundaries of a certain relevant market or for targeting certain geographical districts. Again, one can see how the individual and or household can be left out in this situation.

- Another difficulty presented in defining poverty is that it is *multidimensional*. The challenge is to establish a single index by which a multifaceted problem may be measured.
- Lastly, there is the importance of ensuring that the definition of poverty adequately points to its proper measurements of poverty which in turn indicate the causes of poverty. It is only once poverty is defined, measured, and the causes are properly established, that policies can be established and put in place to alleviate it.

Recognized Approaches to Defining Poverty

In the following section, I will briefly explain the major approaches to defining poverty.

The Income Approach

The time-honoured method of acquiring data to identify the poor and investigate poverty issues is to carry out substantial household surveys that amass information ranging from home expenditures and incomes to the educational attainment and anthropometric measures of members of the household. Either consumption expenditures or income measures typically form the foundation of the welfare measure that is developed to identify the poor. In many studies using household data the minimal standard of living is proxied by the level of consumption expenditure that will enable the household or individual to attain their basic needs – this usually means being able to acquire a selection of commodities containing the minimum quantity of calories and non-food merchandise. All household units not able to attain this crucial level of consumption expenditure or income are categorized as poor.

This approach to defining and measuring poverty can be traced back to the pioneering work done by Charles Booth and Seebohm Rowntree.

In 1885 Charles Booth was angered by the claims of H. H. Hyndman, the leader of the Social Democratic Federation, that 25%[60] of the population of London lived in abject poverty, not to mention that approximately only 5% of them were receiving relief.[61] Inspired by the rioting poor and Hyndman's claims, Booth embarked upon an investigation into the occurrence of pauperism in the East End of the city. Booth's study identified eight social classes, four of which represent different degrees of poverty. His system identified certain aspects beyond income, aspects like sociological concerns and the nature and regularity of employment.[62] The results of his study, *Labour and Life of the People*, revealed that the situation of pauperism was significantly worse than previously

---

[60]H. Hyndman. *The Record of an Adventurous Life* (London: Macmillan, 1911) p. 331.

[61]C. Booth. "The inhabitants of Tower Hamlets (School Board Division), their condition and occupations." *Journal of the Royal Statistical Society* (1887) 50: pp. 326-340.

[62]T. Marshall. *The Right to Welfare: and Other Essays.* (London, Heinemann Educational, 1981), p. 34.

expected. Some 35%[63], and not 25%, of the people were living in abject poverty.[64]

Rowntree's work, which took place in 1899, was attributed as the first scientific study of poverty. The primary objective of his study was both to ascertain the proportion of the population living in poverty and to determine the nature of that poverty.[65] He divided the population into two classes: 1) Families whose total earnings were insufficient to obtain the minimum necessities for the maintenance of merely physical efficiency (primary poverty) and 2) families who would be self sufficient regarding maintenance of physical efficiency were it not that some segment of their earnings was being absorbed by other expenditure (secondary poverty).[66] In order to measure the proportion of the population living in poverty, Rowntree established a poverty line which constituted a minimum amount of income necessary to ensure a "nutritionally" adequate diet, clothing and rent. The results of his study revealed that far more people were in a state of poverty than was originally thought. This information further supported Booth's earlier findings.

Modern income approaches to measuring poverty contain many elements first established through the trials carried out by Booth and Rowntree. Rowntree's method, in particular, still remains in use today, albeit, with a number of adjustments.

Today, most income definitions of poverty are defined with respect to being able to achieve a certain standard of living. Ravallion states that "poverty can be said to exist in a given society when

---

[63]Charles Booth. *Autobiography.* Spartacus Educational. (2002).
[64]Charles Booth. Archive (2002). Available [Online] at: http://booth.lse.ac.uk/static/a/2.html#viii
[65]S. Rowntree. *Poverty: A Study of Town Life.* (London: Macmillan, 1901), p. 9-10.
[66]Ibid.

one or more persons do not attain a level of economic well-being deemed to constitute a reasonable minimum by the standards of that society"[67]. The World Bank defines this form of poverty as "the inability to attain a minimal standard of living" and distinguishes it from inequality, which "refers to the relative living standards across the whole society"[68] Poverty as per these definitions can thus be characterized by the failure of individuals, families or societies to acquire enough resources to satisfy their basic needs.[69]

Most income based approaches tend to denote a specific level of income per capita in a household below which the families' basic needs cannot be satisfied.[70] Poverty definitions that are solely income based are advantageous from the standpoint that they make classifying the poor into one of two categories:

- People who have an income below the poverty line, and
- People who have an income above the poverty line.

Furthermore, according to Sen, a) although the income approaches definition of nutritional requirements might be a little loose, there is no particular reason why the concept of poverty cannot be a little more loosely defined itself, nutritional standards are vague at the best of times, b) in order to check whether someone is receiving the required bundle of nutrition, one need not evaluate whether the person has sufficient income to generate that level of nutrition. One can simply determine whether the person is meeting the specific nutritional standards or not, and c) the income approach focuses emphasis upon malnutrition, and although

---

[67]M. Ravallion. *Poverty Comparisons.* (Harwood Academic Publishers: Switzerland, 1994), p. 3.

[68]*World Development Report.* (New York: World Bank, 1990), p. 26.

[69]J. May. *An Elusive Consensus: Definitions, measurement and analysis of poverty.* (2000).

[70]A. Marshall: Ed. *The State of World Population 1996 report.*

malnutrition is not the only element constituting poverty, it is certainly central to poverty.[71]

The main disadvantages of income based definitions are: "That they impose an official's or observer's view of necessities … and do not acknowledge variation in costs of similar goods for different consumers. The vital importance of non-market household production and non-monetarized exchanges in poor families is not counted. Furthermore, these types of approaches beg the question of how basic needs are defined and by whom, what is an 'accepted' minimal standard of living, and who determines what is acceptable."[72] (My emphasis).

Social Exclusion

Social Exclusion (SE) came about in the late 1970's, first appearing in France and was specifically used to describe the process of marginalisation and destitution which was occurring in wealthier countries with social services in place. It has since spread to the rest of Europe and the UK and is commonly utilized by both social scientists and politicians. The British Prime Minister described SE as: "A shorthand label for what can happen when individuals or areas suffer from a combination of linked problems such as unemployment, poor skills, low incomes, poor housing, high crime environments, bad health and family breakdown."[73]

Townsend, in his earlier work, described this form of deprivation as occurring when people are excluded from ordinary living

---

[71]A. Sen. *Poverty and Famines: An Essay on Entitlement and Deprivation.* (New York: Oxford Press, 1981), pp. 13-14.

[72]A. Marshall: Ed. *The State of World Population 1996 report.*

[73]House of Commons Scottish Affairs. *Poverty. First Report.* 12 July 2000. Available [Online] at http://www.parliament.the-stationery-office.co.uk/pa/cm199900/cmselect/cmscotaf/59/5902.htm

patterns, customs and activities.[74] Le Grand identified SE more precisely as when a person is a part of society, but for some reason beyond their control is unable to participate in normal day to day activities which are typically afforded to citizens of that society, but would like to.[75] Atkinson has gone on to identify certain characteristics of SE:

- Relativity, i.e. that exclusion is relative to a specific society.
- Agencies, i.e. people are typically excluded as a result of the action/s of an agent/s.
- Dynamics, i.e. implying that future prospects are pertinent as well as current conditions.[76]

Figueroa elaborates on the definition of SE by stating that it can be defined in three spheres:
- Economic exclusion takes place when members of a society can no longer participate in the productive economic system, i.e. they are excluded from the labour, credit and insurance markets.
- Political exclusion arises when a legitimate authority fails to guarantee the rights of a person. These rights could fall under any one of the following categories:
  - Civil, i.e. essential personal freedoms such as freedom of residence, expression of belief, ownership, and right to property.
  - Social and economic, i.e. basic education and health,

---

[74]P. Townsend. *Poverty in the United Kingdom.* (London, Harmondsworth: Penguin, 1979), p. 31.
[75]T. Burchardt, J. Le Grand, et al. *Social exclusion in Britain 1991-1995. Social Policy and Administration* (1998), 33(3): p. 229.
[76]A. B. Atkinson. "Social exclusion, poverty and unemployment. Exclusion, Employment and Opportunity." London, London School of Economics. Case Paper 4, Centre for Analysis of Social Exclusion. (1998).

employment, social security, and housing.

- Cultural exclusion can be interpreted in two ways: the marginalisation of specific groups that do not hold fast to the basic codes to interact within the community (ethical values, language, the ability to read and write) and the discrimination against individuals considered to be inferior.[77]

SE tends to differ from other definitions of poverty in that its primary focus is on key target groups like the aged, handicapped, racial and ethnic categories and not the individual.

Some advantages of SE include:

- That it lends itself to the study of the structural characteristics of society (e.g. ethnic minorities, the landless), which can cause and/or characterise exclusion.
- Focus upon distributional issues – "the situation of those deprived relative to the norm generally cannot improve without some redistribution of opportunities and outcomes"[78]
- The fact that it is a dynamic process - which means that it is highly integrated.
- That it is multi-dimensional - and therefore incorporates a wide range of important factors.[79]

Some disadvantages of SE include:

- That it is the least well defined approach.
- That it is probably the most difficult to interpret. Applying the SE approach in developing countries is especially difficult

---

[77]A. Figueroa, T. Altamirano, D. Sulmont, "Social Exclusion and Equality in Peru", *International Institute for Labour Studies, Research Series 104,* 1996, p. 1.

[78]Ibid.

[79]A. Sen. *Poverty as capability deprivation.* (1999). Available [Online] at: http://www.ulandslaere.au.dk/NOTICES/GroupWork/QuestionsAndAnswers2004/Questions_2004/QuestionsFor_5March.htm

because "normality" is difficult to define in multipolar societies, and because there can be disagreement between what is considered normal and desirable.[80]

Poverty as Capability Deprivation

Sen, the brain-child behind "Capability deprivation" (CD) defines it as "the capabilities that a person has, that is, the substantive freedoms he or she enjoys to lead the kind of life he or she has reason to value".[81] What this means is that poverty must be interpreted as deprivation of basic capabilities rather than merely as lowness or lack of income, which is the common criterion for identifying poverty. CD is about increasing people's opportunities and spans both the physiological and sociological realms of deprivation. Thus CD does not only identify the impoverished state in which the person actually lives, but also the lack of real opportunity – due to social constraints as well as personal circumstances – to lead valuable and valued lives.[82]

Capability deprivation can be broken down into three types of deprivation, viz.

- Social Capability Deprivation – deprivation to access to the basis of household production, such as information, knowledge and skills, participation in organizations, and sources of finance.

- Political Capability Deprivation – this occurs when an individual is deprived of access to political decision-making,

---

[80]C. Laderchi, R. Saith, F. Stewart. *Everyone agrees we need poverty reduction, but not what this means: does this matter?* (Paper for Wider Conference on Inequality, Poverty and Human Well being. Helsinki, 30-31 May 2003.), p. 24.

[81]A. Sen. *Development as Freedom.* (Oxford: Oxford Press, 1999), p. 87.

[82]UNDP, Human Development Report, (New York: Oxford Press, 1997), p. 16.

which does not only refer to the capability to vote, but also voice aspirations and collective action.

- Psychological Capability Deprivation – this is deprivation of an individual's sense of his own potential, in the social and political arena, causing him to become incapable of critical thought because he has been indoctrinated by false consciousness. Accordingly, room for critical thought has been destroyed, so no alternative thoughts arise.[83]

The CD approach provides an alternative way of conceptualising individual behaviour, assessing wellbeing and identifying policies for poverty alleviation.

According to Laderchi, Saith and Stewart, there are a number of contributions and difficulties which the CD approach offers to defining poverty. Contributions include:

- First, a support for poverty analysis because it offers a logical framework for defining poverty in the context of the lives people live and the freedoms they enjoy.
- Second, (CD focuses) attention being focussed on a broader range of causes of poverty and options for policies which can alleviate that poverty than do other poverty approaches.
- Third, (CD shifts) compared to the shifting of the emphasis onto the "quality/type of life individuals can live" rather than just onto "quantity of private resources" owned by people.

Some of the difficulties/disadvantages of this approach include:

- Defining the basic capabilities. The problem here lies in that Sen, when formulating his approach to poverty, did not identify a set of minimal essential capabilities which could be used to measure poverty levels. Some pioneering work has been

---

[83]*International Human Resource Development Congress. Attacking poverty through private public partnerships.* Islamabad, October 1-2, 2004.

conducted by Nussbaum in which she has attempted to establish a universally applicable list which can measure the concept of the human being and what is required to be fully human.

See Nussbaum's list below:[84] [85]

Category	Elaboration
Life	Normality with regard to duration of lifespan
Health	Good health, sufficient nutrition and shelter
Bodily Integrity	Free range of movement and choice of reproduction
Senses	Imagination and thought, enhanced by education
Emotions	Relational attachments
Practical reason	Critical reason and planning life
Affiliation	Social interaction; protection against discrimination
Other species	Respect for and living with other species
Control	Over one's environment, politically (choice) and materially (property)

[84]M. Nussbaum. *Women and Human Development: A Study in Human Capabilities.* (Cambridge: Cambridge University Press, 2000), p. 131.
[85]One problem with this list is that the characteristics which it uses to define "full human life" are very general and it also does not specify cut off points which indicate the point of deprivation.

- Measuring the capabilities. Capabilities, as Sen understands them, represent potential outcomes (achievements which a person may attain) and as a result are problematic to identify empirically.
- Determination of the poverty line. As is the case with many poverty measurements, a poverty line is required to separate the poor from the non-poor. In the case of capabilities, a poverty line should be established for each one. The problem is that these poverty lines appear to be context dependent and subjective.
- Aggregation. As a result of the multidimensional approach of CD, aggregation becomes particularly important. The problem is that by aggregating all of the various capability results, one ends up concealing vital information, which in turn hampers analytical and policy formulation efforts.[86]

The Participatory Poverty Approach

The Participatory Poverty Assessment (PPA) approach, first developed by Chambers, differs from the other three approaches discussed in this chapter in that it is the only one which attempts to evaluate poverty from an internal perspective.

It is an iterative, participatory research process that seeks to understand poverty in its local, social, institutional, and political contexts, incorporating the perspectives of a range of stakeholders and involving them directly in planning follow-up action. While *the most important stakeholders involved in the research process are*

---

[86]C. Laderchi, R. Saith, F. Stewart. "Everyone agrees we need poverty reduction, but not what this means: does this matter?" (Paper for Wider Conference on Inequality, Poverty and Human Well being. Helsinki, 30-31 May 2003.), pp. 20-21.

poor men and women, PPAs can also include decision makers from all levels of government, civil society, and the local elite in order to take into account different interests and perspectives and increase local capacity and commitment to follow-up action. Because PPAs address national policy, micro-level data are collected from a large number of communities in order to discern patterns across social groups and geographic areas.[87]

Historically, PPA developed from Participatory Rural Appraisal (PRA) which can be defined as "a growing family of approaches and methods to enable local people to share, enhance and analyse their knowledge of life and conditions, to plan and to act."[88]

PPA's were initially developed by Chambers to operate on a small scale as an attempt to alleviate pockets of poverty torn areas. However, the World Bank saw the value in this method and adopted it as part of their method of evaluating entire countries in terms of poverty conditions. The World Bank began accumulating the voices of some 60,000 poor women and men from 60 countries, in an unprecedented effort to understand poverty from the perspective of the poor themselves. *Voices of the Poor*[89], as this PPA initiative is known, records the struggles and desires of poor people for a life of dignity.

According to the World Bank, poor people are the true poverty experts. Poor men and women reveal, in particular, that poverty is multifaceted and very involved -- raising new challenges to local, national and global decision-makers. "Poverty is voicelessness. It's

---

[87]The World Bank Group. *Participatory Poverty Diagnostics.* (2004).

[88]R. Chambers. *The origins and practice of PRA. World Development* (1994), 22(7).

[89]N. Deepa with R. Patel, K. Schafft, A. Rademacher and S. Koch-Schulte. 2000. "Voices of the Poor: Can Anyone Hear Us?" Chp. 2, *Definitions of Poverty.* New York, N.Y.: Published for the World Bank, Oxford University Press.

powerlessness. It is insecurity and humiliation, say the poor across five continents."[90]

To grasp the essence of poverty, World Bank researchers visited poor urban and rural communities and facilitated discussions on four issues:

- What is a good life and bad life?
- What are the poor people's priorities?
- What is the nature and quality of poor people's interactions with state, market and civil society institutions?
- How have gender and social relations changed over time?

Contextual methods of analysis are involved: i.e., data collection methods, which "attempt to understand poverty dimensions within the social, cultural, economic and political environment of a locality".[91]

Some of the advantages of the PPA include:

- The fact that externally imposed standards are minimised.
- It assists other poverty approaches with their measurements, e.g. this method assists in defining the minimum basket of commodities for the monetary approach and the basic capabilities in the capability approach and whether SE makes sense in a particular society as well as what the main aspects of SE are.
- This method provides the clearest perspective of that of the poor people themselves.
- The method is apparently cost effective.

Some of the problematic issues facing the PPA approach include:

---

[90]The World Bank Group. *Poverty Net. What is Voices of the Poor?* (2004).
[91]B. David, J. Holland, et al. *Participation and Combined Methods in African Poverty Assessments: Renewing the Agenda.* (London, DFID Social Development Division Africa Division, 1998), p 52.

- Even though the poor are the target of the research, it always ends up being the outsiders (the scientists and statisticians) who end up interpreting the results. This leaves room for a skewing of the results.
- PPA are conducted with the intention of carrying out some form of poverty alleviation plan. The problem is that on numerous occasions, the relation between the participatory exercise and the proposed project is very remote.
- Heterogeneity within the community poses a further problem. The question is "Whose voices are actually being heard?" For example, if there are conflicts within the society, it becomes impossible to arrive at a consensus on poverty related matters, and further more, there might even be fearfulness amongst some of the people if they speak out.
- There is the situation that some of the people are not heard. These are the people who do not have social relations with the rest of the community and almost always end up being the poorest of the poor.
- Yet another problem is that poor people's own assessment of their condition can overlook their objective condition and can be biased as a result of limited information and social conditioning (i.e., these methods also suffer from 'physical condition neglect' and 'valuation neglect'.)[92]
- Finally, the exercise of conducting these trials is very time consuming.

---

[92]C. Laderchi, R. Saith, F. Stewart. "Everyone agrees we need poverty reduction, but not what this means: does this matter?" (Paper for Wider Conference on Inequality, Poverty and Human Well being. Helsinki, 30-31 May 2003.), p. 27.

A Working Definition of Poverty

Having considered these different approaches to poverty, I would like to offer my own definition of poverty:

> It is a complicated multifaceted state which has at its very core the word "lack" in terms of all things essential for material security – particularly in regard to numerous resources leading to physical deprivation.

Keeping this definition in mind, I would like to point out that while my definition focuses on physical deprivation, the outcome of assisting people physically tends to be positive on a mental and spiritual poverty scale as well. One must not forget that human dignity is also closely intertwined with poverty and the experience thereof. I will touch on this aspect later as it impacts on the methods we use to help the poor.

That brings us to the end of this chapter and Section A. In the following section, I will focus on the biblical language of social justice.

SECTION B

The Biblical Language of Social Justice

Introduction

In Section B, I am going to turn to the scriptures for knowledge and wisdom on the matter of the poor. The Chapters will be ordered as follows: 1) An outline of the biblical terminology for the poor, 2) The poor as a sociological group, 3) Special classes of the poor, 4) General evidence of concern for the poor, 5) God's concern for special classes of the poor, 6) God's response to the poor, and finally 7) The Christian's response to the poor.

Before we begin on our biblical journey though, it is important to be aware that there is confusion about the "nature" of the Kingdom of God within different Christian theologies. I would not have mentioned this, but for the fact that it has played a damaging role in how different circles within Christianity approach personal and social ethics, particularly in regard to poverty and the poor.

Confusion over the Nature of the Kingdom of God

The subject of "the Kingdom of God" was Jesus' most emphasized topic, but what is it?

Different movements/churches will tell you diverse things. For example, many in the charismatic movement pursue what is known as "Kingdom Now" theology. This Charismatic Kingdom Theology stresses the connection between the Kingdom of God and spiritual gifts; there is a strong tendency to equate the

Kingdom with the powerful manifestations of the Spirit *only.*

At the other end of the spectrum you will find Liberation Theology, which equates the Kingdom of God with manifested social and political change. In a letter from Cardinal Arns to Fidel Castro, he states in regard to the thirtieth anniversary of the Cuban Revolution, that "Christian faith discovers in the achievements of the Revolution signs of the Kingdom of God." Ratzinger states, in regard to Liberation Theology, that the concept of the Kingdom of God is "read against the background of marxist hermeneutics… the Kingdom must not be understood in a spiritualist or universalist manner, not in the sense of an abstract eschatological eventuality. It must be understood in partisan terms and with a view to praxis. The meaning of the Kingdom can only be defined by reference to the praxis of Jesus, not theoretically: it means working at the historical reality that surrounds us in order to transform it into the Kingdom."[93]

What am I trying to say here? "Some parts of the church focus entirely on 'spiritual' aspects of the Christian life, such as evangelism, conversion, personal sanctification, prayer and the spiritual disciplines, [while] other parts of the church focus exclusively on 'social' aspects of the Christian life, such as compassion for the poor, community transformation, social justice and political advocacy. The former is often described pejoratively as 'pietism' and [the latter]…the 'social gospel.'"[94] This dualism has manifested itself throughout history, and it is seriously erroneous. The subject

---

[93]J. C. Ratzinger, "Liberation Theology." A "private" document, which preceded the *Instruction of Fall* 1984. Joseph Ratzinger is presently Pope Benedict the XVI.

[94]Morphew in Q. J. Howitt, and D. J. Morphew. *The Kingdom, Human Dignity and the Poor: A Biblical Ethic of Social Justice.* Unpublished course offered through The Vineyard Bible Institute. 2006, p. 11.

has been addressed by Lovelace.[95] His book looks at scriptural principles, examines past revivals, and establishes a theologically sound model for implementing the lessons learned from the scriptures and the wisdom of the past. Drawing much upon Jonathan Edwards, Lovelace proposes that the elements of revival are: conviction of sin, deep understanding of justification, and movement of the *Spirit,* prayer, community, missions, & *social compassion* (My emphasis).

You will notice from his list that dualism is bridged to emphasize both the spiritual and social aspects of the Kingdom of God.

What then is the Kingdom of God?

"The Kingdom of God is not simply about having 'Jesus in your heart' or having his Lordship 'within you,' a popular definition based on Luke 17:21.[96] Neither is the Kingdom of God merely about the eternal rule of God 'up there' in heaven where he is enthroned. The Kingdom is an event. It is about God 'coming' in the eschatological moment when the powers of the coming age break into the present, in Jesus, in Pentecost and in the history of missions, finally to be manifest when we arrive at the 'end of the end.' Jesus is the personified focus of this Kingdom event. He comes announcing the Kingdom and demonstrating the Kingdom and then enacts the Kingdom through his death, resurrection and ascension. Within this context, the duality of personal spirituality and social ethics is not conceivable. When John the Baptist sent his delegation, wondering if Jesus was really 'the one' Jesus' reply was to evoke the language of Isaiah. Jesus replied, 'Go back and report to John what you hear and see: The blind receive sight, the

---

[95]R. Lovelace, *Dynamics of Spiritual Life: An Evangelical Theology of Renewal,* InterVarsity Press, 1979.

[96]"Within you" is probably better translated as "in our midst," referring to the fact that Jesus was there in their midst, announcing and demonstrating the kingdom.

lame walk, those who have leprosy are cured, the deaf hear, the dead are raised, and the good news is preached to the poor. Blessed is the man who does not fall away on account of me' (Matthew 11:4-6)." Not only do we find the signs and wonders aspect (healing and the raising of the dead) side by side with the message to the poor, but the "good news to the poor" forms the climax to the signs of the Kingdom. At another pivotal moment, when Jesus inaugurated his Kingdom message, he actually quoted Isaiah (Luke 4:4-20). Clearly, Jesus viewed his mandate as somehow an enactment of expectations in Isaiah."[97]

Keeping this understanding of the nature of the Kingdom of God in mind, I now return to consider the biblical language of social justice.

---

[97]Morphew in Q. J Howitt and D. J Morphew. *The Kingdom, Human Dignity and the Poor: A Biblical Ethic of Social Justice.* Unpublished college course offered through The Vineyard Bible Institute. 2006, p. 12.

Bibilical Terminology for the Poor

Let us begin our biblical journey on the topic of the poor by considering various synonyms used to describe them in both the Old and New Testaments. There are quite a few of them and each will add to our understanding of who these people were in ancient times. You might find as you work through this chapter that there are classes of people classified as "poor" that you had never thought of before.

Old Testament Scriptural Words for the Poor [98]

- The most common word used for the poor in the Old Testament is *āni* or *ānāw*, which means "poor, weak, afflicted, or humble." [99] It occurs 92 times in the Old Testament and is likely to be the underlying word for *ptōchós* in the New Testament. [100] *Āni* most likely derives from the root *'nh* (II) which means to be "bent, bowed down or afflicted". It implies

---

[98] I would like to indicate my indebtedness to Kittel, Friedrich and Bromiley in this section.

[99] H. Botterweck and H. Ringren. *Theological Dictionary of the O.T.*, I–III, 1974ff. VI, pp. 888–902.

[100] G. Kittel, G. Friedrich, & G.W. Bromiley. *Theological Dictionary of the New Testament*. Translation of: *Theologisches Worterbuch zum Neuen Testament*. W.B. (Grand Rapids, Mich: Eerdmans Publications, 1995). CDROM Galaxy Software. Hereafter referred to as *TDNT*.

a person who has been dehumanized, oppressed or reduced to some form of diminished capacity.

- Closely associated with *ānī* and *ānāw* is *ebyôn,* economically or legally distressed; destitute, beggarly, from the root 'bh (II), which means "to be willing, to consent". The word occurs 61 times in the Old Testament and generally connotes "poor in a material sense." [101]

- Yet another common word used for the "poor" in the Old Testament is *dal,* "one who is low" from the root *dll,* which means "to languish, to be weak, to be little." It occurs 48 times in Scripture and is often used as a parallel to *ānī* (Amos 2.7; Isaiah 10.2; 11.4; Proverbs 22.22) or to *ebyôn* (Amos 4.1; 8.6; Isaiah 14.30; 25.4). [102]

- The fourth word used for "poor" is *rāš,* the root word implying "destitution". It occurs 32 times. The root points to the circumstances common to the "lower class". Nathan used this term in his parable to illustrate David's sin (2 Samuel 12:1ff). [103]

- The fifth synonym for "poor" is *miskēn.* This word occurs only in Ecclesiastes 4:13; 9:15–16. The scarce use of *miskēn* makes it problematical to draw exact conclusions about its meaning, although the general meaning is obvious in the contrast between the poor man and the king (Ecclesiastes 4:13) – the young man can rise out of the prison of poverty while the king is in danger of falling into poverty.

- The sixth word used for "poor" is *mahsôr* and usually connotes "lack of, or need for, material goods". It occurs 13 times in

---

[101] Ibid.
[102] Ibid.
[103] R. L. Harris, G. L. Archer & B. K. Waltke. *Theological Wordbook of the Old Testament* (Chicago: Moody Press, 1999). CDROM Galaxy Software. Hereafter referred to as TWOT.

Scripture, most of those occasions being in Proverbs where it refers to those who are poor as a result of "laziness" (Proverbs 6.11; 14.23; 21.5; 24.34) or "excessive living" (Proverbs 21.17).[104]

New Testament Scriptural Words for the Poor

The widespread use of numerous terms to denote the poor in the Old Testament is not the case in the New Testament, where the poor are to be understood in a more limited and literal sense. The most common term for the poor in the New Testament is *ptōchós* from the root *ptōssō* meaning to "crouch or to cringe." The word thus connotes a person who is utterly "destitute", "mendicant" and must beg for a living.[105] It is used a total of 34 times.

All of the other terms for "poor" in the New Testament occur just once each. There is *pénēs*[106] used to describe Christ's relinquishment of His glory to take on "poverty" (2 Corinthians 8.9) and the related *penichrós* (Luke 21.2) meaning "very poor," "needy," "wretched" (Luke 22.2);[107] *endeēs* (Acts 4.34) from the root *endeō*, on the other hand, simply refers to somebody who has a need.

One can see from this brief summary of the words used for "poor" plus their frequency of use that the "poor" play a large role within Scripture. In fact, as Soares – Prabhu states: "No other religious tradition I know of gives such importance to the poor or assigns to them such a significant role. For the Bible does not just merely present the poor as deserving of human concern ... nor does it merely point to the plight of the poor as warning against

---

[104]Ibid.

[105]*TDNT.*

[106]In Greece the most common term was *pénēs* and was used of the man who did not have extensive possessions, and had to work for his living. *TWOT.*

[107]*TDNT.*

wastefulness and sloth ... the Bible's main concern is to reveal the theological significance of the poor, the part they have to play in saving history."[108]

At the end of each section from here on out, I have included some questions to aid you in grappling with the subject. I encourage you to ponder on them and use them to engage further discussion on the plight of the poor.

For Reflection

This chapter has focused upon the terminology used in both the Old and New Testaments for the poor.

1. What is the benefit of knowing all these terms?
2. Could you relate these categories of the poor to the society in which you live? Which would fit and which would not?

---

[108]G.M. Soares-Prabhu. *Class in the Bible: The Biblical Poor of a Social Class? Interpreting the Bible in the Third World,* (Maryknoll New York: Orbis Books, 1991), p. 153.

The Poor as a Sociological Group

In this chapter, I will look at the poor as a sociological group. I will do so by investigating the Old Testament, followed by the New.

The Old Testament

According to Soares-Prabhu, the poor in the Old Testament were first and foremost the sociologically poor. They were the economically impoverished and the socially exiled. It is these sociologically poor who learnt from their hopelessness to place their trust in God. The poor in spirit were thus also the materially poor.

More specifically, "the poor" encompasses the following defined groups:

The Destitute

The *ebyôn*, who could be found in both rural and urban environments, were on the lowest rung of the ladder. They included the unemployed landless labourers – artesian and beggars, slave labour (they had been indebted and could not afford to repay their debts) – all those who possessed nothing and had to get by through beggary or through relief afforded by a socially aware community system (Leviticus 19.9, 23.22).

We see in the prophetic corpus that they were characterized by physical insecurity and homelessness (Isaiah 14.30; 25.4; Amos

8.4); hunger and thirst (Isaiah 32.6-7; 41.7; Ezekiel 16.49); exploitation by the rulers of society and other evildoers (Isaiah 29.19; Jeremiah 2.34; 20.13; Ezekiel 18.12; 22.29; Amos 4.1); unjust handling of legal issues (Isaiah 32.7; Jeremiah 5.28; 22.16; Amos 5.12); and economic manipulation (Amos 2.6; 8.6).

The Psalms portray them as those who were robbed (Psalm 35.10), those who suffer (Psalm 107.41) and those who are victims of the swords and bows of the wicked (Psalm 37.14). The wisdom texts speak out about there being some who "devour the poor" (Proverbs 30.14 NKJV). In Job they are portrayed as victims either of economic injustice (Job 24.4) or murder (Job 24.14). In Esther, they are the recipients of alms (Esther 9.22). Clearly, this was a group who were landless and living on the fringes of society.

The Peasant Farmer

The *dal*[109] included the indigent and indebted peasants who lived in severe economic anguish, without being totally impoverished or marginalized. These people, most likely, still owned some land (Proverbs 13.23) and as a result were liable to taxation, in particular, unfair grain taxes paid to large landowners (Exodus 30.15; Leviticus 14.21).

We see in the prophetic corpus that they too were susceptible to unfair treatment in legal disputes (Isaiah 10.2; 11.4; Jeremiah 5.28); suffered abuses in the debt-slavery system (Amos 8.6); a lack of grazing land (Isaiah 14.30; Jeremiah 39.10); and exploitation and oppression of an undefined character (Amos. 2.7; 4.1). *Dal*, at least in the prophetic texts, referred to the economically and politically marginalized people in society.

In the narrative and legal texts, a clear picture of the *dal* is

---

[109] Please refer to the heading entitled "Scriptural words for the poor" for an explanation on *dal*.

conjured up by its use in describing the emaciated cows in Pharaoh's dream (Genesis 41.19). This is probably what flashed before the typical Israelites eyes when considering this group in society.

The Psalms allude to unfairness in matters of the law, for God calls on the legislative body to judge the *dal* justly (Psalm 82.3).

The wisdom literature describes this form of poverty as one that is "the destruction of the poor" (Proverbs 10.15 NKJV); it is a foe which, when it comes to "friends", "drives them away" (Proverbs 19.4 NLT). Lastly, when one evaluates the body of texts containing the word *"dal,"* it is possible to conclude that they are somewhat agricultural in nature and might have been small farmers.

The Afflicted and Oppressed

The *āni* are primarily those people suffering some kind of disability or distress.[110] They are generally afflicted or oppressed, not only economically.

In the prophetic literature one sees oppression in an economic form (Isaiah 3.15; Ezekiel 18.12; cf. Deuteronomy 24.12; Ezekiel 22.29; Amos 8.4), unfair treatment of legal decisions (Isaiah 10.2); and persecution through deception (Isaiah 32.7). Furthermore, society's leaders are said to have robbed the poor of their possessions (Isaiah 3.14) and Ezekiel actually attaches the destruction of Sodom to its inhabitants' failure to look after their poor (Ezekiel 16.49; cf Genesis 18.16-19.29). One of the most noteworthy uses of the word *āni* in the prophetic texts occurs in Isaiah 40-66. Here the *āni* are the oppressed poor Israelites caught up in the Babylonian exile. According to earlier prophets, the Israelites were taken into exile because they oppressed others. Thankfully for the Israelites, this judgment was temporary (Isaiah 51.21;

---

[110] *TWOT* and G.B. Gray, *Isaiah International Critical Commentary* (Poole: T&T Clark Publishers, 1995), p. 310.

54.11 cf. 48.9-10). The *ānī* are described by Isaiah as searching for water but finding none (Isaiah 41.17) and are portrayed as being homeless (Isaiah 58.7).

In the Psalms the *ānī* are depicted as being hounded and seized upon by the wicked and mighty (Psalm 10.2, 9; 14.6; 35.10; 37.14; 106.16) or being ransacked (Psalm 12.6). The *ānī* are homeless (Psalm 25.16), murdered with bows and swords (Psalm 37.14) and in immense physical pain (Psalm 69.30).

In the wisdom texts the lot of the *ānī* is disastrous (Proverbs 15.15). The writer of Proverbs encourages the student not to "crush the *ānī* at the gate" (Proverbs 22.22 NRS) which implies that the wise were mistreating the poor in a legal sense. Later in Proverbs, we see the *ānī* being devoured by the power-holders of society (Proverbs 30.14). In Job, the suffering of the *ānī* is very tangible: they are forced into hiding (Job 24.4); their children are seized as a pledge (Job 24.9; 2 Kings 4.1-7); and they are murdered (Job 24.14). The *ānī* were those who cried out (Job 29.12). The *ānī* were those who had no real estate.[111]

Those in Need or the Poor

The term *mahsôr* is mainly used in the wisdom literature and usually connotes those people who were poor because they had been lazy (Proverbs 6.11; 14.33; 21.5; 24.34) or had lived an excessive lifestyle (Proverbs 21.17). Little else is known of them.

The Economically and Politically Inferior

The term *rāš* most commonly referred to that class of people who were known as the economically poor, of modest means or who were beggars. The majority of its appearances occur in the wisdom

---

[111]A. Ralphs. "Âni und 'ânâw in den Psalmen," *Theol. Diss.* Göttingen 1891-92, Nr. 8 — Leipzig: A. Pries, 1891 {46 S. – 8}, pp. 74-75.

texts where it connotes poverty resulting from laziness (Proverbs 10.4) and need that arises from disordered living (Proverbs 13.23). It is also seen as a friendless form of poverty (Proverbs 14.20; 19.7; 28.3). At least in one text the person can possibly be depicted as a beggar (Proverbs 18.23) because they are described as petitioning the rich for assistance.

In the historical narrative, the most vivid picture of the rāš appears in Nathan's parable to David where the *rāš* is pictured as a poor person who owns only one small sheep (2 Samuel 12:1-4).

The Pious Poor

In a limited number of texts, mostly from the post-exilic times, the "poor" in the Old Testament can mean the "spiritually poor", the "poor of God", who trust in God alone (Isaiah 66.2; Zephaniah 3.12). This is predominantly true of some exilic and post-exilic psalms, in which the original sociological meaning of *ānāwîm* has been so overlaid by the spiritual that it is often impossible to distinguish between the two (Psalm 22.24; 34.6; 86.1; 140.12-13).[112] There are however only a few passages which clearly evidence the circumstances of the *ānāwîm*. They are those who lack food (Psalm 22.27); they are the landless (Psalm 37.11); and they are in pain (Ps 69.33). One specific text describes the opponents of the *ānāwîm* as being the wicked (Psalm 147.6). In the prophetic literature the *ānāwîm* have become the victims of social injustice (Isaiah 32.7; Amos 2.7; 8.4).

The New Testament

Under the following section the subject matter will include an attempt to systematically work through those books of the New

---

[112]R.S Sugirtharajah. *Voices from the Margin. Interpreting the Bible in the Third World* (Maryknoll New York: Orbis Books, 1991), p. 153.

Testament which focus on the "material and physical" use of the word *ptōchós* to paint a picture of this sociological group.[113]

James

According to Hanks, the book of James is the New Testament writing, which stands closest to the Old Testament prophet's viewpoint on poverty and oppression.[114] Those to whom James wrote were very likely not destitute (James 2.2), but they certainly were not wealthy (James 2.6). Stegemann believes them to have consisted of small farmers and artisans who had very little and had to live sparingly.[115] The beggars in the region were characterized by shabby clothing (James 2.2); being naked or lacking daily food (James 2.15-16). They were also the weak, needy, and marginalized, which included women (James 2.15) and the sick (James 5.14-15).

According to Maynard-Reid, it appears as if the oppression of the poor functioned in at least three different ways in James: First, through financial legal mechanisms against the poor debtors – they

---

[113]This book is primarily focussed upon "physical and material lack". However, it must be said that there are occasions where the word *ptōchós* is used to describe the "spiritually poor" (Matthew 5.3; Galatians 4.9; and Revelation 3.17). Furthermore, there appear to be three New Testament texts (Matthew 5.11 and Luke 7.22; Luke 4.18 and Luke 6.20) where the meaning of *ptōchós* is uncertain and in dispute. It is unsure as to whether these verses point to the "spiritually poor whose religious attitude of openness and trust disposes them to receive God's love *Or* ... are they the sociologically poor whose situation of social deprivation invites God's saving action on their behalf?" (My emphasis). R.S Sugirtharajah. *Voices from the Margin. Interpreting the Bible in the Third World* (Maryknoll New York: Orbis Books, 1991), p. 155.

[114]T. D. Hanks. *For God so loved the Third World* (Maryknoll, New York: Orbis Books, 1983), pp. 45-50.

[115]W. Stegemann. *The Gospel and the Poor* (New York: Fortress Press, 1984), pp. 40-41.

were being dragged into court (James 2.1-12, cf. 2.6); second, the greedy merchant class (James 4.13-17); and third, the rich agriculturalists were withholding the wages of the poor (James 5.1-6).[116]

James tries to envision a community who live a lifestyle which reaches out to the destitute above all else even though they live within a society typified by greed, domination and oppression of the poor and weak (James 1.8; 21; 4.6; 5.19-20).[117] Furthermore, James attempts to curb the sin of the "tongue" which denies dignity, respect, and justice to the poor class in their community (James 2.6-7).

Finally James emphasizes "being a doer of the word" when it comes to helping the poor. Failing to do this is tantamount to murdering them (James 5.6) and committing adultery with the world (James 4.4-6).

Mark

Ptōchós is used in three contexts in Mark (Mark 10.21, the rich man; Mark 12.42-43, the widow's mite; Mark 14.5, 7, and the anointing at Bethany). However, there appear to be numerous indirect references to poverty, especially in the lives of John the Baptist (Mark 1.6; 6.17, 27), Jesus (Mark 6.3; 11.12; 14.65; 15.15, 19), the voluntary deprivation of both groups of disciples (Mark 1.18, 20; 2.23-25; 6.8-9, 36-37; 9.41; 10.28-31)[118] and the socio-economic level of those who followed Him.[119] Stege-

---

[116]P.U. Maynard-Reid. *Poverty and Wealth in James.* (Maryknoll NY: Orbis Books, 1987), pp. 48-98.

[117]E. TamEzekiel *Faith without Works Is Dead. The Scandalous Message of James.* (Bloomington: IN, 1989), pp. 56-69.

[118]J. C. Parrares. *A Poor Man Called Jesus: Reflections on the Gospel of Mark* Trans. R Barr. (Maryknoll, NY: Orbis Books, 1986), p. 176.

[119]C. Myers. *Binding the Strong Man: A Political Reading of Mark's Story of Jesus.* (Maryknoll, NY: Orbis Books, 1988), p. 120.

mann concludes that "the movement within Judaism in Palestine associated with the name of Jesus was a movement of the poor for the poor".[120] It is likely that many of the people in Mark's time were not at the level of destitution. However, most of them were barely avoiding poverty.[121]

Luke

Luke's emphasis on the poor should be placed in the context of his general focus on previously disadvantaged or rejected groups, Gentiles, women, children and sinners. He has deep concern for the "immoral minorities" (Luke 7.2, 34, 37, 39).[122]

Luke's version of the beatitudes is striking when compared to Matthew's. "Jesus promises to those who are needy and downtrodden that they will experience a reversal of their present unhappy lot, and threatens the rich and prosperous with the loss of their present possessions" (Luke 6:20-26).[123]

In Matthew the emphasis is on spiritual poverty. When Jesus berates the Pharisees for cleaning only the outside of the cup, where Matthew has "First clean the inside of the cup and dish, and then the outside also will be clean" (Matthew 23:26), Luke has "But give what is inside the dish to the poor, and everything will be clean for you" (Luke 11:39).

In the Magnificat Mary praises God because "He has put down the mighty from their thrones, and exalted those of low degree; he

---

[120]W. Stegemann. *The Gospel and the Poor.* (New York: Fortress Press, 1984), p. 23.

[121]H.C. Waetjen. *A Reordering of Power: A Socio-Political Reading of Mark's Gospel.* (Minneapolis: Fortress, 1989), pp. 10-11.

[122]L. W. Countryman. *Dirt, Greed, and Sex: Sexual Ethics in the NT and their Implications for Today,* London: IVP, 1989, pp. 66-74.

[123]I. Howard Marshall, *Luke, Historical and Theologian,* Paternoster, 1970, p 141.

has filled the hungry with good things, and the rich he has sent empty away (Luke 1:52). The rich fool is warned of the reversal of his lot (12:13-21). Jesus tells the rich young man, "You still lack one thing. Sell everything you have and give to the poor, and you will have treasure in heaven. Then come, follow me" (18:22).

The parable of those seated at the table, and who find themselves reversed in their positions (14:7-11), is not simply about dining etiquette, but about the messianic banquet. This is born out by the exhortation on banquets. "When you give a luncheon or dinner, do not invite your friends, your brothers or relatives, or your rich neighbors; if you do, they may invite you back and so you will be repaid. But when you give a banquet, invite the poor, the crippled, the lame, the blind, and you will be blessed. Although they cannot repay you, you will be repaid at the resurrection of the righteous" (14:12-14).

The rich are told to "sell your possessions and give alms" (12:33). Clearest of all is the parable of the rich man and Lazarus which has this climax, "Son, remember that you in your lifetime received your good things, and Lazarus in like manner evil things; but now he is comforted here, and you are in anguish" (16:25).

The poor widow makes the greatest contribution because "she out of her poverty put in all she had to live on" (21:1). The sign of the change in Zacchaeus' life is that he gives half his possessions to the poor (19:8).

Luke's emphasis should not be taken as a simple antagonism to the rich. The key issue, in his vision of Jesus' teaching, is the attitude towards God. The rich fool is told: "So is he who lays up treasure for himself, and is not rich toward God" (12:21). This attitude has its context in the coming of the kingdom. The "now" and "then" of the reversal in the beatitudes is about the arrival of the future age.

It follows that the call to discipleship is a call to a lifestyle that has implications for ones attitude to possessions. The disciples leave their homes to follow Jesus (5:11,28; 18:28) and have to make a decisive break with the past (9:57-62), including renouncing all that they had (14:25-33). The earliest Christian community was one where the disciples sold their possessions and distributed them to all who were in need (Acts 2:44f; 4:32). As the gospel spreads it has a particular effect on the poor. It is a crippled beggar who is miraculously healed (3:1-10). A most frightening sudden death occurs to a couple who pretend to give their possessions but lie about it (5:1-10), which at the least shows that one should not trifle with ones heart attitude towards issues of wealth and possessions. The controversy around Stephen has to do with the provisions for widows (6:1-7). Tabitha who was miraculously raised through Peter's ministry is one "who was always doing good and helping the poor" (9:36). The angel says of Cornelius, "Your prayers and gifts to the poor have come up as a memorial offering before God" (10:4). Peter tells Cornelius, "God has heard your prayer and remembered your gifts to the poor" (10:31). Luke obviously wants to make a point here. The church in Antioch makes a significant contribution to the church in Jerusalem during the famine, partly because there were many poor in the Jerusalem community (11:27-30).

The Pauline Letters

Very little is mentioned sociologically about the *ptōchós* in the Pauline letters. One particular passage (2 Corinthians 6:10, cf. 6.3-9) lists Paul's afflictions, where he describes his own life as *ptōchós*. The list is representative of the types of injustices suffered by all those who are *ptōchós*, with poverty and deprivation featuring strongly. The remaining uses of the term appear in Romans

15.26 and 2 Corinthians 8-9 and specifically deal with Paul's collection for the poverty stricken Jerusalem church.[124]

There have been other studies conducted on the socio-economic level of the Pauline churches which reveal that many of the early Christian communities were made up predominantly of "the little people" *(pénēs)* including neither the destitute *(ptōchós)* nor the wealthy.[125] However, there is evidence of the clash between the rich and the destitute in cities like Corinth where the wealthy would get drunk (1 Corinthians 11.21) and go ahead and eat before those who were hungry and had nothing (1 Corinthians 11.22) had arrived for the Lord's Supper (1 Corinthians 11.23-33; cf. 11.17-22). Other areas like the "spiritual gifts" (1 Corinthians 12 and 14) and the need for "love" (1 Corinthians 13) are also better understood under the guise of the socio-economic struggle which existed between the rich and the poor.

For Reflection

At the beginning of this section it states, "They were the economically impoverished and the socially exiled."

1. What are the biggest areas of need within the poor communities nearest you?
2. What does "socially exiled" mean to you and what forms does it take within your needy communities?

---

[124]K. Nickle. *The Collection: A Study in Paul's Strategy,* SBT 48. London, 1966, p. 121.

[125]G. Theissen. *The Social Setting of Pauline Christianity: Essays on Corinth.* Trans. J. H. Shütz. (Philadelphia: Fortress Press, 1982); W. A. Meeks. *The First Urban Christians: The Social World of the Apostle Paul.* (Binghamton, NY: Yale University Press, 1983).

Special Categories of the Poor

"Poverty" was a state that could occur in any person's life. However, apart from those who had fallen into poverty, there were certain groups that were powerless for reasons beyond poverty. Gowan suggests that "in a society which depended so heavily on human muscle power for subsistence, a family without one adult male; composed of a widow and her children, would find it difficult to survive."[126] For the same reasons, orphans faced a similar plight. Further, "the sojourner received a great deal of attention in the Old Testament ... their circumstances could be precarious since they were of foreign origin. Our term "alien," especially when modified by "illegal," immediately suggests to us some of the problems the sojourner faced in Israel."[127] These three are the "special categories" I will focus on in this chapter.

---

[126]D.E. Gowan. "Wealth and Poverty in the Old Testament. The Case of the Widow, the Orphan, and the Sojourner," *Interpretation,* Vol. 41, NY: 1987, p. 343.
[127]Ibid.

The Widow in the Old and New Testament

The Old Testament

The Hebrew word rendered "widow" is *almānā*,[128] which occurs fifty-six times.[129] The allocation of the term "widow" occurs approximately one-third of the time in legal literature, one-third in prophetic literature, and one-third in wisdom and historical literature. However, the bulk of the contexts are legal in nature, dealing with justice (legislation protecting the widow) or injustice (exploitation of her standing). The term refers to a married woman whose husband has died and then remains unattached (2 Samuel 14:2, 5, NRS "Alas, I am a widow; my husband is dead"). The first occasion for its use is in (Genesis 38:11). The account of Judah's dealings with his daughter in-law, who is called a "widow" following her husband's passing. Widows, along with the fatherless and sojourners, were the most vulnerable and dependent class of people in the land.[130]

The subject matter includes words closely associated within the semantic domain of the term "widow" in Scripture in order to shed light on her personal experience and social dilemma. Words like "lamentation" (Job 27:15; Psalm 78:64), "mourning" (2 Samuel 14:2), and "brokenness" (Lamentations 1:1) are descriptive of her personal experience having lost her husband. "Poverty and lack" (Ruth 1:21; 1 Kings 17:7–12) and "indebtedness" (2 Kings 4:1) could describe her economic state, when the main source of her

---

[128] *TWOT.*

[129] The Septuagint virtually always translates *almānā* with the Greek term for widow, *chēra* (cf. Job 24:21). The same Greek word occurs twenty-six times in the New Testament. *TWOT.*

[130] G. Smith. "A Closer Look at the Widow's Offering," The Theological Journal Library CD Version 5, *Journal of the Evangelical Theological Society 2002,* Electronic Edition Volume 40:1, p. 35.

financial support, her husband, had died. She was often associated with the orphan, the landless immigrant (Exodus 22:21–22; Deuteronomy 10:18; 24:17, 19, Isaiah 1:23; Jeremiah 5:28; Job 22:9; 24:3, Lamentations 5:3), the poor, (Isaiah 10:2; Zechariah 7:10), and the day-labourer (Malachi 3:5) as being representative of the dregs of society (Job 24:4; 29:12; 31:16; Isaiah 10:2) in the social structure of ancient Israel. She had little, if any, inheritance rights, and could be described as being in a veritable "no-man's land." The situation was grave indeed, she had left her family when she married, and with her husband's passing, the relationship which existed between her and his family was unstable.

An Israelite widow was especially at risk and dependent because of her inability to provide for herself. In agrarian Israel it was necessary to own and work the land for one's rations. A woman without a husband or sons (particularly if she were advanced in age) would have been unable to support herself (e.g. Naomi in Ruth).[131]

With regard to the remarriage of widows, the only restriction imposed by the Mosaic law had reference to the contingency of one being left childless, in which case the brother of the deceased husband had a duty to marry the widow (Deuteronomy 25:5, 6).

One of the main plights of this group centred on the lack of their "legal rights" (Ezekiel 22:7; Isaiah 1:23; 10:2; Jeremiah 5:28). To the sorry legal and social state of widows corresponds their low esteem among men. This status is reflected in the expression "sorrows of widowhood" (Isaiah 54:4 NLT), the proud saying: "I shall not sit as a widow, nor shall I know loss of children" in Isaiah 47:8 (NAS) and the corresponding threat of widowhood and the equally despised childlessness (Isaiah 47.9).[132]

---

[131]Ibid., p. 36.

[132]Childlessness was a disgrace; the worst fate to befall a woman was to be

Widows had certain restrictions placed upon them. They could not marry priests (Leviticus 21:14: Ezekiel 44:22) unless they were widows of priests. However, widows who were daughters of priests were allowed to return to their father's home in order to eat again of the holy food of the priests (Leviticus 22:13).

The New Testament

The Greek word for "widow" is *chēra*. This word is derived from a root meaning "forsaken," and it most likely refers to any woman living without a husband. Later we also find *chēros* for "widower." The verbs *chēróō* and *chēreúō* mean "to make a widow" and "to become a widow." We also find the derived noun *chēreía*, "widowhood."[133]

Widows in the New Testament generally found themselves in the same precarious situation as those of the Old Testament. Once again, their lives were marred by many injustices. In Mark 12:40 and parallels, Jesus is portrayed as prophetically denouncing the scribes who ostensibly were helping widows with their rights while at the same time charging such high fees that the widows were losing their possessions. Jesus continues this focus through his comment on the widow who, through her trust and devotion, gives her whole living, meagre though this is (Mark 12:41ff). Then there is the parable told in Luke 18:2ff., which further illustrates that issues of a financial and legal nature and widowhood were synonymous with one another.

In early church times there was a hint of more difficulties endured by widows. Acts 6:1 NAU states, "Now at this time while the disciples were increasing in number, a complaint arose on the part of the Hellenistic Jews against the native Hebrews, because

---

sent back to her father's house a childless widow. *TWOT.*
[133] *TDNT.*

their widows were being overlooked in the daily serving of food."

Apparently many Jews of the dispersion would retire to Jerusalem and leave their widows behind. Since the Palestinian believers managed the common funds, they had a propensity to neglect Hellenist widows as tension developed between the native group and the dispersion element. Thankfully this tension was relieved by the intervention of the apostles and the appointment of seven deacons.[134]

Lastly, the pastoral letters as well as James mention a number of rules and regulations which were instituted in an attempt to protect and care for widows. These will be discussed under the section dealing with the concern for the poor.

The Orphan and Fatherless in the Old and New Testament

The Old Testament

The Hebrew word for the Orphan and Fatherless is *yātôm*.[135] It implies a person who has been deprived of their parents. Words associated with it include "desolate", "without protectors", and "comfortless". *Yātôm* is first used in the Bible in the earliest law code of ancient Israel, the Covenant Code in Exodus 22.22. The *yātôm* were generally associated with the "widow" and the "sojourner" and were of special concern to God.[136]

Orphans and the Fatherless had occasion to mourn over and above the normal grief associated with the loss of parents. They lived within the confines of corrupt societies, where the leaders were "often rebellious companions of thieves, acceptors of bribes,

---

[134]Ibid.

[135]*TWOT.*

[136]Evidence of this can be found under the heading entitled *General evidence of concern for the poor.*

and unjust toward orphans and fatherless."[137] There is evidence throughout Scripture of the orphans and fatherless being over-whelmed (Job 6.27), their donkeys being driven away (Job 24.3), their being snatched from the breast (Job 24.9), being murdered (Psalm 94.6), not being defended and their cause not pleaded (Isaiah 1.28; Jeremiah 5.28), being robbed (Isaiah 10.2), and being generally mistreated (Ezekiel 22.7).

Although they had occasion to mourn for all of the above reasons, they were not excluded from the pilgrim festivals: "And you shall rejoice before the LORD your God, you and your son and your daughter, your male servant and your female servant, the Levite who is within your towns, *the sojourner, the fatherless, and the widow* who are among you, at the place that the LORD your God will choose, to make His name dwell there. You shall re-member that you were a slave in Egypt; and you shall be careful to observe these statutes. You shall keep the Feast of Booths seven days, when you have gathered in the produce from your threshing floor and your winepress. You shall rejoice in your feast, you and your son and your daughter, your male servant and your female servant, the Levite, *the sojourner, the fatherless, and the widow* who are within your towns" (Deuteronomy 16.11-14 NAU).

The New Testament

The Greek word for orphan and fatherless is *orphanós* and it means "bereaved," "without parents or children". Occasionally it is used in the figurative sense and means "abandoned," or "deprived".[138] It is used only twice, the first in James 1:27, in a literal sense to describe the kind of behaviour which should be afforded orphans

---

[137]J. H. Fish III. "The Commission of Isaiah., *Emmaus Journal,* Volume 4:1 (Summer 1995), p. 50.
[138]*TDNT.*

and fatherless and the second, in John 14.18, in a figurative sense, to demonstrate Jesus not leaving the disciples "orphaned", i.e. "abandoned" or "unprotected".

The Sojourner in the Old and New Testament

The Old Testament

The Hebrew word for "sojourner" is *gēr*, which refers to someone who lived permanently within a land but did not enjoy the rights typically possessed by a resident of the land. To further clarify, the root word for *gēr is gûr*, which means to live among people who are not blood relatives; therefore, rather than benefiting from indigenous civil rights, the *gēr* was reliant upon the generosity that formed an important role in the ancient near east.[139] The alternative *tôšā* (sojourner) occurs fourteen times, this noun refers to the temporary, landless wage earner.[140] The term is used with *gēr* (permanent resident, alien) to describe Abraham in Canaan (Gen 23:4), as well as the Israelites in God's eyes (Leviticus 25:23, 35; Psalm 39:12; 1 Chronicles 29:15). It is also used as a synonym for a "hired servant" (Exodus 12:45; Leviticus 22:10; 25:40).

A good example of the noun *gēr* can be seen when used to describe Israel's sojourn in Egypt: "Then the LORD said to him, 'Know for certain that your descendants will be strangers in a country not their own, and they will be enslaved and mistreated four hundred years' " (Genesis 15:13; Exodus 23:9). Another

---

[139] *TWOT.*

[140] *TWOT,* besides the "permanent versus temporary" residence difference between the *gēr* and the *tôšāb*, there was also the matter of the *tôšāb* not being allowed to participate in the eating of the Passover as well as the fact that his children could be sold into slavery (Leviticus 25:45). However, like the *gēr*, he could still seek the protection of the cities of refuge (Numbers 35:15).

example is that of Moses when he named his son "Gershom" in memory of his stay in Midian, "and her two sons, of whom the name of the one is Gershom, for he said, 'a sojourner I have been in a strange land' " (Exodus 18:3 YLT). Lastly, Abraham, Isaac and Jacob were "sojourners" in Canaan (Exodus 6:4) implying that they lacked property rights there.

The sojourners in Israel were typically considered as proselytes. They were included in the Israelite legal system (Leviticus 24:16, 22; Numbers 35:15; Deuteronomy 1:16) and were required to be present for the reading of the Law (Deuteronomy 31:12), thereby showing their exposure to its demands. They were subject to many of the religious requirements, namely the laws of ritual cleanliness (Leviticus 17:8-13; but cf. Deuteronomy 14:21), keeping of the Sabbath and fast days, celebrating the Day of Atonement (Exodus 20:8-10; 23.12; Leviticus 16:29) and the Feast of Booths (Deuteronomy 16:14.). Passover could be celebrated by the proselytes if they were circumcised (Exodus 12:48-49; Numbers 9:14). Furthermore, they could offer sacrifices (Numbers 15:14-16, 29). Along with the natives, sojourners were threatened with death if they dared offer a sacrifice to a foreign god (Leviticus 17:5f.). They were also forbidden to eat blood (Leviticus 17:10, 12, 13). Sojourners were allowed to eat what had died or was torn which was not the case for the resident (Deuteronomy 14:21), and like the resident Israelite, they had to undergo special cleansing (Leviticus 17:15f.).

Proselytes were also included in the red heifer rites of cleansing (Numbers 19:10). The same laws of sexual chastity applied to them as did to the residents (Leviticus 18:26). In a word they were to show the same fidelity to God as did the native (Leviticus 20:2). Finally, Ezekiel even foresaw a time when sojourners would be granted an inheritance in the land, implying citizenship (Ezekiel 47:22-23).

The New Testament

The word more commonly used for "sojourner" is "alien." In secular Greek there are three terms for "alien" namely: *pároikos* (a. "neighbouring," "neighbour," and b. "noncitizen," "resident alien"); *paroikía* (resident alien); and *paroikéō* (to live as a resident alien).[141] *Pároikos* occurs four times, *paroikía* twice, and *paroikéō* twice, most of the uses being allusions to the Old Testament:

- "But God spoke to this effect, that his descendants would be aliens in a foreign land, and that they would be enslaved and mistreated for four hundred years" (Acts 7.6 NAU).

- "The God of this people Israel chose our fathers, and exalted the people when they dwelt as strangers in the land of Egypt, and with an uplifted arm He brought them out of it" (Acts 13.17 NKJV).

- "By faith he made his home in the promised land like a stranger in a foreign country; he lived in tents, as did Isaac and Jacob, who were heirs with him of the same promise" (Hebrews 11.9 NIV).

- "All these people were still living by faith when they died. They did not receive the things promised; they only saw them and welcomed them from a distance. And they admitted that they were aliens and strangers on earth" (Hebrews 11.13 NIV).

- In similar fashion to that of the Israelites, the Christians were aliens but had become citizens in a new family, "so now you Gentiles are no longer strangers and foreigners. You are citizens along with all of God's holy people. You are members of God's family" (Ephesians 2.19 NLT).

In similar fashion to Israel, Christians were and still are "aliens" in the world: "Dear brothers and sisters, you are foreigners and aliens

---

[141] *TDNT.*

here" (1 Peter 2.11a NLT).[142] The church as *ekklēsia* is *paroikía*. It is *ekklēsia* relative to God, but *pároikia* relative to the world (Hebrews 13:14).[143]

In conclusion, Soares-Prabhu states that "all through the Bible ... the poor *in all its categories* are a sociological ... group. Their identity is defined ... by their sociological situation of powerlessness and need"[144] (My emphasis). He goes on to mention that Biblical poverty is wider in scope than mere economics, that it includes all those who are in any way deprived of the means or the dignity they need to lead a fully human existence. The poor are "the wretched of the earth", the exploited and the oppressed.[145]

For Reflection

1. How are widows, orphans and non-residents perceived within your society? Is there any special care provided for each of these respective groups by the state? The same question applies to your church and yourself.
2. How do you think God would want these groups to be treated? "Religion that is pure and undefiled before God, the Father, is this: to care for orphans and widows in their distress, and to keep oneself unstained by the world" (James 1.27 NRSV).
3. Are there any timeless scriptural principles you could apply?

---

[142]Compare also Jesus' allusion to the disciples not being part of the world, "They are not of the world, even as I am not of it" (John 17.16 NIV.)

[143]*TDNT.*

[144]G.M. Soares-Prabhu. *Class in the Bible: The Biblical Poor of a Social Class? Interpreting the Bible in the Third World,* Maryknoll New York: Orbis Books, 1991, pp. 156-157.

[145]Ibid., p. 157.

General Evidence
of Concern for the Poor

If the amount written about a topic within a book is any indication of the importance of that topic to the author, then "concern for the poor" ranks very highly on God's list. From cover to cover, the bible is littered with God's policies, rules and regulations about them. I will investigate these by considering firstly, various preventative commands, principles, and laws and secondly, warnings concerning the poor.

Preventative Provisions

It is evident from Scripture that a number of principles or laws were instituted which, if applied, would prevent massive class distinctions and poverty from arising. The distinctions could not be hidden but the poverty could be alleviated by some of these provisions. These included:

The Jubilee Principle

Through the year of Jubilee (Leviticus 25.8-55) God desired to achieve a revolution in the Israelite society every 50 years. Its purpose was to avoid extremes of wealth and poverty amongst His people. Jubilee provided for restoration of the prior status in most instances.[146]

The basic points of the laws were as follows:

- Freedom for all the slaves and debtors (Leviticus 25.40-41). A parallel here would be Israel's flight from Egypt depicted in the exodus (Leviticus 25.38).
- Restitution of each clan's patrimony – a type of agrarian reform accompanied by the redistribution of wealth. "This year will be set apart as holy, a time to proclaim release for all who live there. It will be a jubilee year for you, when each of you return to the lands that belonged to your ancestors and rejoin your clan" (Leviticus 25.10 NLT). This reminds one of the conquests of Canaan and equitable distribution of the land as described in Joshua.
- Rest for the land, allowing it to lie fallow (Leviticus 25.11).

All of these provisions of the law related to freedom (of debtors, slaves, property, and even the land). Ezekiel referred to this time as "the year of freedom" (Ezekiel 46.17 NIV). The Jubilee made Israel re-experience the events recorded in Exodus and Joshua.

The theological basis for this controversial command was that all of their possessions actually belonged to God and were merely on lease so that they might be good stewards of them.[147] "Land will not be sold absolutely, for the land belongs to me, and you are only strangers and guests of mine" (Leviticus 25.23 NJB).

Before and after the year of Jubilee the land could be bought or sold. However, the buyer did not actually buy the land so much

---

[146]T. D. Hanks. *For God so loved the Third World,* Maryknoll, New York: Orbis Books, 1983, p. 113.

[147]C.L. Blomberg. *Neither Poverty nor Riches: A Biblical Theology of Material Possessions,* Grand Rapids, Michigan and Cambridge, U.K.: Eerdmans Publishing, 1999, p. 40.

as he bought a certain number of harvests,[148] "When the years are many, you are to increase the price, and when the years are few, you are to decrease the price, because what he is really selling you is the number of crops" (Leviticus 25.16 NIB).

The year of Jubilee imagined an institutionalized structure that affected everyone automatically. It also allowed for self-help and self-development. With his land returned to him, the poor person could once again earn his own living. The Biblical principle of the Jubilee emphasized the significance of institutionalized devices and structures that encourage justice.[149]

The Sabbatical Year

The Jewish sabbatical year was in effect a religiously mandated fallow year for all fields.[150] It was also a law allowed for the liberation of slaves and debtors every seven years.[151]

For six years you are to sow your fields and harvest the crops, but during the seventh year let the land lie un-ploughed and un-used. Then the poor among your people may get food from it, and the wild animals may eat what they leave. Do the same with your vineyard and your olive grove (Exodus 23.10-11 NIB; cf. Leviticus 25.2-7).

It is believed that the purpose for this was two-fold:[152]

- *Environmental*: By not planting in the seventh year the

---

[148]R.J. Sider. *Rich Christians in an Age of Hunger: A Biblical Study,* London, Sydney, Auckland, Toronto: Hodder and Stoughton, 1973, p. 79.

[149]Idid. p. 80.

[150]D.E. Oakman. *Jesus and the Economic Questions of His Day,* Lewiston and Queenston: The Edwin Mellen Press, 1986, p. 27.

[151]R.J. Sider. *Rich Christians in an Age of Hunger: A Biblical Study.* (London, Sydney, Auckland, Toronto: Hodder and Stoughton, 1973), p. 81.

[152]R. de Vaux, *Ancient Israel,* London: Darton, Longman and Todd, 1973, pp. 173-175.

fertility levels of the land were preserved; and

- *Concern for the poor:* God was ensuring that the poorest of the poor would be able to eat (Exodus 23.10-11).

Israelite slaves also received their freedom every seventh year (Deuteronomy 15.12-18). They had become slaves because of poverty. Selling oneself to pay off debts, and in some cases, simply to keep from starving, was a common trend in ancient times (Leviticus 25.39-40). However, God decreed that slavery was not to be permanent: "if any who are dependent on you become so impoverished that they sell themselves to you ... They shall serve with you until the year of the jubilee" (Leviticus 25.39-40 NRS).

Finally, the sabbatical provision on loans was the most radical of all (Deuteronomy 15.1-6). God decreed that every seven years, all debts had to be cancelled (Deuteronomy 15.1). God even added that people were not allowed to refuse loans in the sixth year simply because the money would be lost in twelve months (Deuteronomy 15.9). As was the situation with the year of Jubilee, the sabbatical year was brought about to ensure justice and not charity. The relief of debts was an institutionalized device for curbing an ever increasing gap between rich and poor.[153] Sider goes on to mention that Deuteronomy 15 was both "an idealistic statement of God's perfect demand and also a realistic reference to Israel's probable performance concerning debts."[154] God knew, however, that the ideal of having no poor in the land would not happen, hence the statement "Since there will never cease to be some in need on the earth, I therefore command you ..." (Deuteronomy 15.11a NRS). But, this did not imply that He would allow everyone to go on with their lives and their business in total ignorance of the poor. On

---

[153]R.J. Sider. *Rich Christians in an Age of Hunger: A Biblical Study,* London, Sydney, Auckland, Toronto: Hodder and Stoughton, 1973, p. 81.
[154]Idid. p. 82.

the contrary, His instituted law meant that those with means were expected to "Open your hand to the poor and needy neighbor in your land" (Deuteronomy 15.11b NRS). Sadly, there is evidence which suggest that the sabbatical year was only practiced occasionally, which was one of the reasons why God punished Israel with exile in Babylon (Leviticus 26.35-36; 2 Chronicles 36.20-21).[155]

Laws on Tithing and Gleaning

There were additional laws to those mentioned above, which, if practiced, were designed to aid specific groups, such as the Levite, as well as the poor, the sojourner, the widow and the orphan. One such law was that of setting aside one tenth of all farm produce, whether wine, animal or grain as a tithe:

At the end of every third year you shall bring out the tithe of your produce of that year and store it up within your gates. And the Levite, because he has no portion nor inheritance with you, and the stranger and the fatherless and the widow who are within your gates, may come and eat and be satisfied, that the LORD your God may bless you in all the work of your hand which you do (Deuteronomy 14:28-29 NKJV).[156]

There is a strong likelihood that these surplus supplies would have been kept in storehouses (Leviticus 27.30-32; Deuteronomy 14.27-29; 26.12-15; Numbers 18.21-32; 1 Chronicles 26:15, 17; Nehemiah 10:38, 44; 13:12-13; and Malachi 3:10).

Another law, the law of gleaning, decreed that farmers should leave some of their harvest, including the corners of their fields, untouched so that the poor could go and glean there: "When you

---

[155]R. de Vaux, *Ancient Israel*, London: Darton, Longman and Todd, 1973, pp. 173-175.
[156]L. P. Moore, Jr. "Prayer in the Pentateuch Part 3," *Bibliotheca Sacra* Vol. 99, Dallas Theological Seminary 393, Jan, 2002, p. 112. CDROM Galaxy Software.

reap the harvest of your land, you shall not reap your field right up to its edge, neither shall you gather the gleanings after your harvest. And you shall not strip your vineyard bare; neither shall you gather the fallen grapes of your vineyard. You shall leave them for the poor and for the sojourner: I am the LORD your God" (Leviticus 19.9-10 ESV; cf. 23.22).

Furthermore, farmers were instructed not to collect forgotten sheaves left in the field, olive tree boughs were not to be "gone over again" and orchards were not to be gleaned after grape collection (Deuteronomy 24.18-21).

Additional Preventative Laws and Commands regarding the Poor

In addition to the commands, laws, and principles mentioned above, further emphasis concerning the "general poor" appears in the following commands:

- Significant emphasis was placed upon ensuring justice for the poor. The Israelites were to guard against perverting the judgment of the poor in disputes (Exodus 23.6), showing partiality (Exodus 23.3), taking bribes (Deuteronomy 10.17), making use of dishonest scales, weights, ephah, and hin (Leviticus 19.36), oppressing the afflicted (Proverbs 22.22), and committing violence (Jeremiah 22.3). Instead, they were to "learn to do good; seek justice, rebuke the oppressor" (Isaiah 1.17 NKJV).
- The area of money lending also provided evidence of care for the poor. The Israelites were prohibited from charging interest on loans (Exodus 22.25) or keeping a person's pledge overnight (Exodus 24.12). Furthermore, collectors of the poor man's pledge were not allowed to enter the houses of those who owed them. They were to stand outside and wait while the man of the house went inside to collect the pledge. This

ensured that adequate respect and dignity for the poor was upheld (Deuteronomy 24.10-11).

- Special conditions were laid down for the cleansing of "poor" healed lepers. Instead of the customary fee, poor lepers were allowed to reduce the size of their trespass offerings for atonement purposes: "But if he is poor and cannot afford it, then he shall take one male lamb as a trespass offering to be waved, to make atonement for him, one-tenth of an ephah of fine flour mixed with oil as a grain offering, a log of oil, and two turtledoves or two young pigeons, such as he is able to afford: one shall be a sin offering and the other a burnt offering" (Leviticus 14.21 NKJV).

- The payment of wages was also mandated. The hired servant who was poor and needy was to be paid his and her wages each day before the sun went down (Deuteronomy 24.13).

Warnings concerning the "Poor"

Besides the numerous laws, commands and principles found in Scripture, there are also a number of warnings given in favour of the poor. These warnings include the following:

- Generally, the poor were a class of people who could fall prey to various forms of abuse more readily than others. Therefore, a warning in the form of a curse was issued to prevent this from happening. "He who gives to the poor will lack nothing, but he who closes his eyes to them receives many curses." (Proverbs 28.27).

- In the section in Proverbs dealing with the Wisdom of Solomon, the Israelites are warned that when one oppresses the poor they are in effect reproaching their Maker (Proverbs 14.31). Those who oppress the poor in order to increase their wealth are also guaranteed of coming to poverty (Proverbs

22.16). Those who shut their ears to the cry of the poor will be cut off from the Lord, "whoso stoppeth his ears at the cry of the poor, he also shall cry himself, but shall not be heard" (Proverbs 21.13 KJV).

• Ezekiel, in the section dealing with the refutation of a false proverb, warns those who oppress the poor and needy of grave consequences: "He oppresses the poor and needy. He commits robbery. He does not return what he took in pledge. He looks to the idols. He does detestable things. He lends at usury and takes excessive interest. Will such a man live? He will not! Because he has done all these detestable things, he will surely be put to death and his blood will be on his own head" (Ezekiel 18.12-13 NIV).

In the section dealing with the "Coming Messenger", the future judgment of Israel appears to include not only the Levites, but the entire nation (Ezekiel 20:34-38).

For Reflection

1. Highlight every principle or law mentioned in this section which assists the poor. Consider which of these principles or laws still apply today? Be careful here, do some in-depth research using good commentaries before you finalise your list.

2. Scripture states that the "Land will not be sold absolutely, for the land belongs to me, and you are only strangers and guests of mine" (Leviticus 25.23 NJB). It is not hermeneutically incorrect to stretch this principle to include all our material possessions. Have you ever thought that all of your material possessions are owned by God? Do you really believe this? You actually have no option if you believe scripture is the Word of God. So how is this going to impact upon your future

lifestyle? Treat these questions with the utmost seriousness.

3. Imagine that you are the law makers of the land: Can you devise any laws you would set in place to help protect the poor (you can use biblical texts, but you will have to contemporise them)?

4. Who, within your community, region, province, state or country, would you approach with these suggested laws? You may want to consider sending your collective suggestions to this/these parties.

5. The year of Jubilee imagined an institutionalized structure that affected everyone automatically. It also allowed for self-help and self-development. With his land returned to him, the poor person could once again earn their own living. Discuss this law within your group.

6. Keep in mind that the Jubilee principle was instituted within an agrarian society. We seldom realize the weight of this principle within our societies. The fact is that if a person in ancient times did not have land, they virtually had no way of earning a living. How could the Jubilee principle be applied today? In those days, land was the key life resource. What is it today?

God's Concern for
Special Classes of the Poor

In chapter five, I covered those classes that were more likely to end up in poverty due to their predicaments, viz. widows, orphans and the sojourner. In this chapter, I will focus again on these classes, but this time from the angle of what God instituted to protect them.

The Widow

The Old Testament includes a significant amount of legislation to protect the widow. She was not to be oppressed (Exodus 22:21–22; Deuteronomy 27:19); she was entitled to a share of the communal tithe (Deuteronomy 14:29; 26:12–13); provision was to be made for her at religious feasts (Deuteronomy 16:9–15); she was allowed to glean the fields and vineyards at harvest time (Deuteronomy 24:19–21, cf. Ruth 2); and her articles of clothing could not be removed from her as security for a loan (Deuteronomy 24:17). Moreover, the ultimate measure by which a ruler in Israel was to be judged was whether he cared for such defenceless ones. One such occasion was when the Lord directed Jeremiah to go to the king with a message of warning. The message was to encourage the king and his entourage to do what was righteous.

Certain consequences would be attached to whichever action the king chose. If he chose to commit no violence toward the widow, amongst others, i.e., to adhere to God's commands, he could expect ongoing blessing. However, if he did not, God promised that his palace would be desolated (Jeremiah 22.3-5, cf. Psalm 72:4, 12–14; Jeremiah 22:16).

The prophets, in particular, were very outspoken about the oppression of widows. For them, penitence began with rectifying wrongs done to such women, "This is what the Lord says: Be fair-minded and just. Do what is right! Help those who have been robbed; rescue them from their oppressors. Quit your evil deeds! Do not mistreat ... widows. Stop murdering the innocent!" (Jeremiah 22.3 NLT, cf. Isaiah 1:17; Jeremiah 7:6; Zechariah 7:10). "The prescribed way of life in the wisdom literature takes care of the weak. It is definitely regarded as the policy of God to protect the widow ... God maintains the borderline of a widow's property" (Proverbs 15.25),[157] and encouraged a compassionate approach regarding widows. Job evidenced great kindness and compassion for widows by never sending a begging widow away without food (Job 29:13).

Widows were also a concern in the New Testament. Jesus revealed a like concern to that of the prophets for the widows' plight. "He delivered the only son of the widow of Nain to his mother, we read in Luke 7:11–16 because He had great compassion on her".[158] He also overturned the benchmark by which people were judged through utilizing the parable of the widow's tithe:

---

[157]F.C. Fenshaw. "Widow, Orphan and Poor in ancient and near eastern legal and wisdom literature," *Journal of Near Eastern Studies,* Vol. 21, 1962, p. 137.

[158]H. Bultema. "Will There Be Recognition in Heaven?" *Bibliotheca Sacra,* Dallas Theological Seminary, Vol. 95:380, October 1938, p. 473. (CDROM Galaxy Software).

the widow gave her all (out of her poverty) while the rich simply presented minute percentages of their wealth (Mark 12:41–42). Furthermore, Jesus objected to the oppression of widows by stating that the scribes were men who devoured "the property of widows and for show offered long prayers" (Mark 12:40 NJB).

The early church defined the heart of "true religion" as demonstrating kindness for those who were poor and needy, especially the widows and the orphans (James 1:27). There is evidence of a specific trust being established for particular groups of widows in the church (Acts 6:1–6; 1 Timothy 5:3–16).

The Orphan

"It is interesting to note that a concern for the ... orphan ... is permanently woven into the fabric of those crucial sections dealing with the covenant made between God, the sovereign, and His people."[159] In fact, this concern is vividly portrayed throughout the Old Testament in a number of ways: God cares for orphans (Psalm 68:5; Hosea 14:3); He considers the oppression of orphans a serious offence (Jeremiah 7:2–7); He defends the orphan (Deuteronomy 10:17–18; Psalm 10:17–18); God assists the orphan in times of need (Psalm 10:14); He prohibits the oppression of orphans (Jeremiah 22:3; Zechariah 7:8, 10); God promises to punish the oppressors of orphans (Exodus 22:22–24; Isaiah 1:23–25; Isaiah 10:1–2; Jeremiah 5:27–29; Ezekiel 22:7, 13; Malachi 3:5); He protects the orphans (Jeremiah 49:11); He provides for the orphans (Deuteronomy 14:28–29; Deuteronomy 26:12–13); and finally, God sustains the orphans (Psalm 146:9). "*In God's name the Old Testament demands that injustice be fought, righteousness be*

---

[159]R. D. Patterson. "The Widow, the Orphan, and the Poor in the Old Testament and the Extra-Biblical Literature," *Bibliotheca Sacra*, Dallas Theological Seminary Vol. 130:519, Jul 1973, p. 229.

established in society, and the orphan, ... the poor, and the oppressed be made the objects of protection and provision."[160] (My emphasis)

In the New Testament there is only one passage of interest. James continues the stance seen in the Old Testament that *the essence of true religion is "to look after orphans ... in their distress"* (James 1.27 NIV).

The Sojourner

"The picture of the believer as sojourner is used repeatedly in the Bible."[161] God laid down numerous regulations in the Old Testament out of concern for the sojourner. Israelites must not oppress them (Exodus 22:21; 23:9; Leviticus 19:33–34). In fact, the Israelites were expected to love the sojourner, "Love the sojourner, therefore, for you were sojourners in the land of Egypt." (Deuteronomy 10:19 ESV, cf. Leviticus 19.34). The gleanings of the vineyard and the harvest were to be left for them (Leviticus 10:10; 23:22; Deuteronomy 24:19–21). The protection of the six asylum cities were also cities of refuge for them (Numbers 35:15; Josh. 20:9). They were classified amongst the orphans and widows as being "defenceless" (Psalm 94:6; Zechariah 7:10). They were virtually on a par with the Israelites (Leviticus 24:22), with a few exceptions: they were excluded from the general liberation of slaves in the year of jubilee (Leviticus 25:45–46), and had no inheritance rights in the land.[162]

By the time of the New Testament, Israel had become

---

[160]C. C. Ryrie. "Perspectives on Social Ethics Part II: Old Testament Perspectives on Social Ethics," *Bibliotheca Sacra*, Dallas Theological Seminary, Volume 134:534, April 1977, p. 115. (CDROM Galaxy Software).

[161]D. F. Gibson. "Applying the New Testament Metaphors. A Case Study: The Alien," *Michigan Theological Journal*, Michigan Theological Seminary, Vol. 1:2, Fall 1990, p. 132. (CDROM Galaxy Software).

[162]Ibid., p. 119.

increasingly elitist, almost forgetting her call to the nations. When Jesus was born, however, sojourners were still evident (Matthew 2.1–12). Significantly, Jesus regularly related to them, demonstrating God's love for the world (Luke 17.18; John 4.9). Through Jesus' death and resurrection, there would no longer be any significant ethnic, gender, or linguistic differences: "For you are all sons of God through faith in Christ Jesus. For all of you who were baptized into Christ have clothed yourselves with Christ. There is neither Jew nor Greek, there is neither slave nor free man, there is neither male nor female; for you are all one in Christ Jesus. And if you belong to Christ, then you are Abraham's descendants, heirs according to promise" (Galatians 3:26–29 NAU).[163]

Early Christians had to come to grips with the truth that while they were members of a gloriously new forming kingdom, they were also sojourners on earth (1 Peter 1.17; 2.11 cf. John 17.14) and would have to continue that nomadic type of existence similar to the patriarchs of old, desiring a better country, that is, a heavenly one (Hebrews 11.9–16).

The church is expected to conduct itself with the utmost courtesy and compassion towards sojourners, keeping in mind her own identity and background and the Lord's love and respect for the powerless: "For I was hungry and you gave Me something to eat, I was thirsty and you gave Me something to drink, I was a stranger and you invited Me in, I needed clothes and you clothed Me, I was sick and you looked after Me, I was in prison and you came to visit Me" (Matthew 25.35-36 NIV).

---

[163]Pentecost (Acts 2) reversed the judgment of the tower of Babel (Genesis 11:1–9).

For Reflection

1. What is a sojourner and who in your society would most closely fit this profile?

2. The biblical teaching clearly eliminates positions of gender, race or class inequality. What are your feelings toward race, gender and class distinctions? Can you honestly say that you have no biases? If you cannot, you have some work to do.

3. Consider the following statement: "Christians had to come to grips with the truth that while they were members of a gloriously new forming Kingdom, they were also still sojourners on earth (1 Peter 1.17; 2.11 cf. John 17.14). This is a radical statement. If you had to choose to live by this standard, in what ways would it begin to impact upon your lifestyle?

4. Consider the following verses: "For I was hungry and you gave Me something to eat, I was thirsty and you gave Me something to drink, I was a stranger and you invited Me in, I needed clothes and you clothed Me, I was sick and you looked after Me, I was in prison and you came to visit Me" (Matthew 25.35-36 NIV). Is your church living up to it? If not, what should you do about it?

God's Attitude Toward the Poor Expressed in Various Stages of Commitment

The previous two chapters have focussed on God's concern for the poor. Before we move on, I would like to raise a valuable insight made by Sugirtharajah concerning God's attitude toward them. He believes that God's attitude can be categorized into *various stages of commitment,* viz.[164]

- *God has a concern for the poor.* He listens to them (Psalm 69.33; 34.6; Isaiah 41.17). He delivers the needy when he cries (Psalm 72.12). He sets them on high, far from affliction (Psalm 107.41). He gives to them (Psalm 112.9; 132.15). He raises them out of the dust (1 Samuel 2.8; Psalm 113.7). He is their refuge and protector (Isaiah 3.13-15; 24.4 ff; 25.4; Zephaniah 3.12; Psalm 14.6). He consoles and comforts them Isaiah 49.13, and He is the helper of the fatherless (Psalm 10.13).

- *God vindicates the poor.* He administers justice for them (Deuteronomy 10.18; Job 36.6; Psalm 10.17; 25.9; 72.4; 82.3; 140.12), delivers them in their affliction (Job 36.15; Psalm 35.10; 72.12; 76.9; 82.3; Jeremiah 20.13), defends the widow,

---

[164]R.S. Sugirtharajah, Editor, *Voices from the Margin. Interpreting the Bible in the Third World,* Maryknoll NY: Orbis Books, 1991, pp.158-159.

the fatherless and the stranger (Exodus 22.21-24; Deuteronomy 10.17-19; Psalm 68.5; 69.5; 82.3), saves the needy from the sword (Job 5.15); and pleads their cause (Isaiah 51.22).

• *God demands a like concern from His people* (Exodus 22.21-24. Leviticus 19.10; Deuteronomy 15.1-11; 24.14f; Isaiah 58. 1-12; Jeremiah 7.5-7; Ezekiel 16. 49; Zechariah 7.10), and from their king (Isaiah 11.4; Jeremiah 22.16; Psalm 22.1-4). Through the prophets He zealously condemns every form of oppression (Amos 2.6-8; 4.1-3; 6.4-8; Micah 2.1-3; Isaiah 3.13-15; 10.1-4; Jeremiah 22.13f; Ezekiel 34.1-24).

God's concern for the poor is so extreme that He goes further than to plead their cause, *He actually identifies with them.* "He who oppresses the poor", Proverbs tells us, "insults his maker" (Proverbs 14.31); while to be "kind to the poor" is to "lend to God" (Proverbs 19.17).[165]

Finally, because God so identifies with the poor, *He sees them as "His people"* (Isaiah 3.15), He extends Himself to punish those who harm them (Job 22.9; Psalm 109.16; Isaiah 1.23-24; 3.13-15; Jeremiah 5.28-29; 22.3, 15-19; Ezekiel 16.48-50; 22.7, 14-15, 29-31; Amos 2.6; 4.1-3; 5.12-16; 8.4-8; Malachi 3.5) and blesses those who are good to them (Job 29.11-17 cf. 42.12-16; Psalm 41.1; Proverbs 14.21; 17.5; 19.17; 29.14; Jeremiah 7.6-7; 22.3).

In chapters three through to seven, I have reviewed *The Biblical concern for the poor.* I will move on from this to consider how God responds to the poor in the following chapter.

---

[165]Ibid.

For Reflection

Sugirtharajah makes an interesting observation concerning *various stages of commitment* demonstrated by God. Where on this scale do you think God's concern for the poor would lie today?

God's Response to the Poor

In this chapter, I will concentrate on certain biblical evidence emphasizing the inherent value of a human being as well as texts capturing Jesus Christ's response toward the poor. This will be done in the hope of identifying how Christians and disciples should respond to them. As has been the case in other chapters, I will investigate from an Old and New Testament perspective.

The Old Testament

A lot of information concerning "the Biblical concern for the poor" was given in the previous chapters, which focused more on the Old Testament rather than the New Testament. In this section only a few key passages from the Old Testament will be discussed before moving on to more applicable teachings found in the New Testament.

The Creation Account

In the beginning, God said, "'Let us make man *in our image, in our likeness*, and let them rule over the fish of the sea and the birds of the air, over the livestock, over all the earth, and over all the creatures that move along the ground.' So God created man in His own image, in the image of God He created him; male and female He created them" (Genesis 1.26-27 NIV) (My emphasis).

Gaebelein states that God's making us in His image is positively one of the greatest things ever said about humanity. Although this image is marred by the fall, it is not beyond God's regenerating power.[166] Considering humankind in this manner emphasizes the fact that a human's dignity springs from God's image and not materialism, status or power. C.S. Lewis captured the implications of this aptly in one of his sermons: "The dullest and most uninteresting person you talk to may one day be a creature which, if you saw it now, you would be strongly tempted to worship, or else a horror and a corruption such as you now meet, if at all, only in a nightmare ... You have never talked to a mere mortal ... *realize that* it is immortals that we joke with, work with, marry, snub, and exploit – immortal horrors or everlasting splendours"[167] (My emphasis).

What has this to do with the subject at hand? Human beings are the "image bearers" of the living God and therefore deserve the utmost levels of respect and dignity. This is totally inconsistent with people suffering from poverty. Those who live in the Western World cannot turn a blind eye on those in need because God will not tolerate it.

When God made humans He "took the man and put him in the Garden of Eden to tend and keep it" (Genesis 2.15 NKJV). Gaebelein suggests that humans received a delegated authority, a subordinate supervisory role for which they were responsible to God. The Biblical principle of the relation of humanity to God's world is not ownership but stewardship.[168] This is clearly reflected in the jubilee principle, "The land shall not be sold in perpetuity, for the land is mine. For you are strangers and sojourners with

---

[166] F. E. Gaebelein, R. J. Sider (Editors), *Old Testament Foundations for Living More Simply*, London: Hodder and Stoughton, 1982, p. 30.
[167] C.S. Lewis. *The Weight of Glory*, New York: Macmillan, 1949, p. 15.
[168] F. E. Gaebelein, R. J. Sider (Editors), *Old Testament Foundations for Living More Simply*, London: Hodder and Stoughton, 1982, p. 31.

me" (Leviticus 25.23 ESV).

The Commandments given at Mt Sinai

Christians need to heed the commandments and precepts laid down by the Lord in Scripture. For instance, the first two commandments state: "You shall have no other gods before me. You shall not make for yourself an idol, whether in the form of anything that is in heaven above, or that is on the earth beneath, or that is in the water under the earth. You shall not bow down to them or worship them" (Exodus 20.3-5a RSV).

This challenges our fundamental outlook. Time and again, the Old Testament repeatedly warns us against the idolatry inherent in materialism. The history of Israel is marred by their love of prosperity and riches and God's judgment upon them. Solomon, the wisest man to ever live, serves as a classic example of the danger of affluence upon a person's life. It clouds a person's vision and can turn them away from their maker.

Another commandment of particular relevance is the tenth: "You shall not covet your neighbor's house; you shall not covet your neighbor's wife, nor his male servant, nor his female servant, nor his ox, nor his donkey, nor anything that is your neighbor's" (Exodus 20.17 NKJV). As Gaebelein notes, it was covetousness which the serpent used in the garden to tempt Adam and Eve to eat from the tree. The temptation was for them to reach out for a lifestyle which the Lord did not create them for. The last commandment probes the sin of progressive aggrandizement that leads Christians, in an already tempting materialistic society, into idolatrous lifestyles in which almost everything is spent on self and only a miniscule amount is given to the needy. There is a process of "wanting more and more" and giving less and less.[169]

---

[169]Ibid., p. 33.

The Old Testament does not provide a detailed, exact list of how we ought to live our lives, but it does provide us with certain principles and precepts which we can use to measure the way we live. It is up to us to face those principles and precepts in all honesty. In doing this, there will almost certainly be a change in the way we live, perceive the needy and utilize our finances.

The New Testament

The pinnacle of human history can be summed up in Jesus Christ being born into this world to usher in the new age. It is therefore vital, as human beings, for us to carefully investigate why He came, and to understand His mission and purpose.

So many Christians seek to know the answer to "what does true Christian commitment and praxis demand." The answer to this may lie in evaluating Jesus Christ's mission, purpose, and teachings regarding the poor.

The Ushering in of a New Age – Jesus Christ's Mission and Purpose

Under this section, extensive reference will be made to the excellent work produced by Hanks in his exceptionally detailed study entitled "God so loved the Third World".[170]

This key text, read by Jesus in the synagogue, clearly portrays His mission and purpose: "The Spirit of the Lord is upon Me, because He has anointed Me to bring good news to *the poor*. He has sent Me to proclaim release to *the captives* and recovery of sight to *the blind*, to let *the oppressed* go free, to proclaim the year of the

---

[170]It is the opinion of the writer that no author he has found has so aptly captured the "Mission and Purpose" of Jesus Christ in such detail. See also T. D. Hanks, *For God so loved the Third World,* Maryknoll, New York: Orbis Books, 1983.

Lord's favor" (Luke 4.18-19 NRS) (My emphasis).

On closer inspection, Jesus' words portray the human situation in shockingly realistic terms, particularly with regard to the developing countries. The following is a close analysis of Jesus' words in His mission statement.

The Poor

Jesus Christ's priority in His mission was to turn His attention to the poor who quite literally dominated the Palestinian population at that time.[171] It is interesting to note that Jesus not only ministered to the poor, He "cast His lot with them".[172] This is evident in a number of ways:

- Jesus was born in a stable to a humble virgin girl,
- Jesus' family was poor,[173]
- Jesus was a refugee,[174]
- He was an immigrant in the land of Galilee;[175] He humbly

---

[171]A very similar case scenario resides in Africa today.

[172]T. D. Hanks, *For God so loved the Third World,* Maryknoll, New York: Orbis Books, 1983, p. 110.

[173]The offering which they presented for her purification showed that they were a poor couple. They could not afford a lamb, so they bought a pair of doves or pigeons, which were all they could afford. "And if she be not able to bring a lamb, then she shall bring two turtles, or two young pigeons; the one for the burnt offering, and the other for a sin offering: and the priest shall make an atonement for her, and she shall be clean" (Leviticus 12.8 KJV)

[174]"And on their having withdrawn, lo, a messenger of the Lord doth appear in a dream to Joseph, saying, 'Having risen, take the child and his mother, and flee to Egypt, and be thou there till I may speak to thee, for Herod is about to seek the child to destroy him.' And he, having risen, took the child and his mother by night, and withdrew to Egypt, and he was there till the death of Herod, that it might be fulfilled that was spoken by the Lord through the prophet, saying, 'Out of Egypt I did call My Son'" (Matthew 2.13-15 YLT).

[175]"After Herod died, an angel of the Lord appeared in a dream to Joseph in Egypt and said, 'Get up, take the child and his mother and go to the land of

submitted Himself to John the Baptist's baptism;[176] Jesus warned a potential follower of the type of life to expect by saying that He had no home.[177]

All of this goes to show that when Jesus addressed the poor, He did so from a position of equality, not from above. Jesus was familiar with suffering, poverty, hunger, mourning and ostracism. The poor and hungry were Jesus' people.[178] Paul the Apostle knew this and summarized all of his teaching regarding the incarnation of Christ in the following words: You know how full of love and kindness our Lord Jesus Christ was. Though He was very rich, yet for your sakes He became poor, so that by His poverty He could make you rich" (2 Corinthians 8.9 NLT).

Israel, for those who were trying to take the child's life are dead.' So he got up, took the child and his mother and went to the land of Israel. But when he heard that Archelaus was reigning in Judea in place of his father Herod, he was afraid to go there. Having been warned in a dream, he withdrew to the district of Galilee, and he went and lived in a town called Nazareth. So was fulfilled what was said through the prophets: 'He will be called a Nazarene'" (Matthew 2.19-23 NIV).

[176]"Then Jesus came from Galilee to the Jordan to be baptized by John. But John tried to deter him, saying, 'I need to be baptized by you, and do you come to me?' Jesus replied, 'Let it be so now; it is proper for us to do this to fulfill all righteousness.' Then John consented" (Matthew 3.13-15 NIV). John was a socialist prophet who challenged the rich to show sincere repentance by sharing their goods with the poor. "The crowd asked, 'What should we do?' John replied, 'If you have two coats, give one to the poor. If you have food, share it with those who are hungry' " (Luke 3.10-11 NLT).

[177]"One of the scribes then came up and said to him, 'Master, I will follow you wherever you go.' Jesus said, 'Foxes have holes and the birds of the air have nests, but the Son of man has nowhere to lay his head'" (Matthew 8.19-20 NJB).

[178]B.D. Chilton. "Jesus and the Jubilee," *The Living Pulpit,* Volume 10 no 2, April-June 2001, pp. 18-19.

The Captives

The oppressed can withstand the pressures of poverty and suffering for a while if there is a light at the end of the tunnel, a way to change the situation.[179] But in 1st century Palestine, as in many third world countries today, the poor and oppressed are trapped in their misery, with no way of improving their situation, no way out.

Furthermore, when one stumbles across the word "prisoners" in the New Testament, it conjures up evocative images of murderers, rapists, bandits and the like. However, in 1st century Palestine, most of the hard core prisoners were executed rather than imprisoned for long periods of time. Most prisoners, therefore, were in prison because they could not afford to pay back their debtors.[180] This implies that when Jesus turned His attention to the "captives and prisoners", He was not considering two separate groups, but one: the poor imprisoned because of debt and poverty.

The Blind

For Jesus to include the "blind" in the same categories as the "poor" and the "captives" means he must have thought of them as part of the same needy group. It is interesting to note that poverty appears in the context as a related circumstance in six of the seven instances that Luke mentions the blind.[181] It could well have been that "blindness" stood for all the sicknesses that the poor suffered

---

[179]Ibid.

[180]See Matthew 5.25-26; Matthew 18.30; Luke 12.57-59. See also C. Westermann, *Isaiah 40-66: A Commentary*, Philadelphia: Westminster, 1969, p. 366. They are not "prisoners of war" as I. H. Marshall claims in *The Gospel of Luke*, Exeter: Paternoster, 1978, p. 184.

[181]Luke 4.18; Luke 7.21, 11; Luke 14.13, 21; Luke 18.35. Also see the year of Jubilee provision (Leviticus 25.35; Isaiah 58.7) for providing a shelter for the poor and homeless mentioned in Luke 14.13, 21. T. D. Hanks. *For God so loved the Third World*, Maryknoll, New York: Orbis Books, 1983, p. 111.

as well as the miserable dependence and the lack of awareness the poor incurred.

The Oppressed

Jesus described the poverty stricken as oppressed, and Hanks' study proves that "oppression" and "injustice" is the number one cause of poverty in the Bible – Old Testament Hebrew uses twenty verbal roots that turn up more than five hundred times to describe oppression.[182] Jesus had come to free the oppressed.

In the face of all this suffering, Jesus bravely offered Himself as the solution to all their terrible suffering and disillusionment. But exactly how did He do this?

The Bringer of Good News

Jesus went about proclaiming the "good news." We should realize the radical nature of Jesus' mandate. The Spirit of the Lord *"was upon Him"* because He was anointed to preach good news to the poor (Luke 4.18 NKJV - My emphasis). One must recall that the proclaimer was the Word, God the Son, who created the universe by His word.[183] With this in mind, one can appreciate the revolutionary impact and power His words would have upon humanity.

The actual "good news" which He came to proclaim was that the Kingdom of God had arrived, ushered in by Himself, through His ministry, in both announcement and demonstration, and through his death and resurrection.[184] Note that it was aimed at the poor!

---

[182]T. D. Hanks. *For God so loved the Third World* Maryknoll, New York: Orbis Books, 1983, p. 111.
[183]See John 1.1-3 and Genesis 1.1 ff.
[184]See 1 Corinthians 15.1-3.

The Proclamation of Freedom

Part of the coming of the Kingdom of God was Jesus' proclamation of liberating the oppressed, "He has sent Me to proclaim freedom *(áphesis)* to the prisoners ..." (Luke 4.18 NIV). According to Hanks, all too often the church has fallen into the trap of legitimizing the oppression that the established order maintains. Christians wish to preach a gospel of socio-political freedom to the poor, whereas others want to offer forgiveness of sins to the rich. Jesus, however, did not offer us the alternative of spreading two gospels. His gospel is one freedom forgiving gospel which is good news to the poor. Of course this is bad news for the rich, unless they genuinely repent, identify with the poor and share their goods with them.[185]

Jesus not only wished to proclaim His message, He actually states that He came to "let the oppressed go free" (Luke 4.18 RSV). This test was inserted into the Isaiah 61.1-2 passage and originates from Isaiah 58.6: "set the oppressed free and break every yoke?" (NIV). As we will see in the coming pages, this phrase has to do with the divine programme of the year of Jubilee.

Recovery of Sight to the Blind

Yet another aspect of Jesus' mission statement was to provide "recovery of sight to the blind" (Luke 4.18 RSV).[186] When John the Baptist was in prison he sent his disciples to find out whether Jesus was the authentic Messiah. Jesus responded: "*Go and report to John ... what ye saw and heard, that blind men do see again, lame*

---

[185]T. D. Hanks. *For God so loved the Third World*, Maryknoll, New York: Orbis Books, 1983, p. 112.

[186]You may recall that earlier on in this section that it was mentioned that "blindness" could have stood for all the sicknesses that the poor suffered as well as the miserable dependence and the lack of awareness the poor incurred.

do walk, lepers are cleansed, deaf do hear, dead are raised, poor have good news proclaimed; and happy is he whoever may not be stumbled in me" (Luke 7.22-23 YLT - My emphasis).

It appears as if the mission statement of Jesus and His followers will always include healing the sick, be it through miracles, through the sensitization of human conscience, or in working to achieve better living conditions for those less fortunate. One must take carefully to heart James' comment that "faith by itself, if it is not accompanied by action, is dead" (James 2.17 NIV).

To Proclaim the Year of the Lord's Favour

This is probably the most dramatic part of Jesus' mission statement. It refers to the year of Jubilee (Leviticus 25), which has already been discussed at length in a previous section on *The Jubilee Principle*. The Jubilee was implemented to prevent massive class distinctions between the rich and the poor. Had Israel followed this law, it could have solved many of the extremes of wealth and poverty occurring in its agrarian society.

Marshall believes that it is even possible that Jesus proclaimed His mission statement in what would have been, had they practised it, the year of Jubilee.[187] Whether this is the case or not, the arrival of the Kingdom of Heaven in Jesus' person put into practice the radical provisions of the Year of Jubilee.

Hanks brilliantly sums up how Jesus preached and taught His disciples how to practice the Jubilee:

- not by sowing, reaping, or harvesting, but by living by faith, always trusting that God will provide for one's needs (Matthew 6.25-26, 31-33; Luke 12.29-31).
- by remitting all debts (Matthew 5.40-42; Luke 6.33; Luke

---

[187]I. H. Marshall. *The Gospel of Luke,* Exeter: Paternoster, 1978, pp. 133, 184.

12.30-33; Luke 16.1-15).

- by redistributing wealth (Luke 11.42; Luke 12.30-33; Acts 2.44-45; Acts 4.32-37).[188]

So far we have dealt with the fact that we are God's "image bearers", and as a result deserve to be treated with the utmost dignity and respect. We have also touched on certain of the Old Testament commandments, which instruct against idolatry of any form (materialism) and covetousness. Lastly, there has been an examination of Jesus Christ's mission and purpose, which clearly lays out His need to concentrate on the poor and needy. Next, attention will be drawn to Jesus Christ's teachings regarding those in need.

A good place to begin this section is to try and grasp God the Father's motivation behind sending Jesus Christ in the first place.

John 3:16 explains this succinctly, "For God so *loved the world* that He gave His one and only Son, that whoever believes in him shall not perish but have eternal life" (NIV - My emphasis). Whether this verse was spoken by John or Jesus, as inspired Scripture it stands as an important summary of the gospel. God's motivation toward people is *love*. That love is not restricted to a select few. His gift is for *the whole world* (Galatians 3.26-29 - My emphasis). God's love was articulated in the giving of His precious Son. In essence, that love was totally sacrificial, outward looking and servant-heart related. It is this love that He expects His disciples to imitate (John 13.34; John 15.12; Romans 13.8, Philippians 2.1-9).

---

[188]T. D. Hanks. *For God so loved the Third World*, Maryknoll, New York: Orbis Books, 1983, p. 114.

For Reflection

1. Discuss your beliefs about the following statement: "A human's dignity springs from God's image and not materialism, status or power." Do you live according to the former or the latter? How do you think your lifestyle would differ by living by either of them?

2. C.S. Lewis makes a profound statement about people in this chapter. It could be summarized as follows: Human beings are the "image bearers" of the living God and therefore deserve the utmost levels of respect and dignity. Live with this thought in the forefront of your mind until you meet again. When you see each other at the next group discussion share with each other how by treating people like this, it has affected your life and the lives of others.

3. This chapter mentions that the last commandment probes the sin of progressive aggrandizement that leads Christians, in an already tempting materialistic society, into idolatrous lifestyles in which almost everything is spent on self, and only a miniscule amount is given to the needy. There is this sense of "wanting more and more" and giving less and less. Think of at least five examples. Additionally, consider whether you have fallen into this trap.

4. Hanks' study proves that "oppression" and "injustice" is the number one cause of poverty in the Bible. Discuss what you think the number one cause of poverty is in your society? Once you have identified it, what can you do to ease it?

5. Jesus preached and taught His disciples how to practice the Jubilee: By living by faith, always trusting that God will provide for one's needs; by remitting all debts and by redistributing wealth. Consider what sort of impact this type of lifestyle (if you or your church lived by it) would have upon society. We

cerebrally believe that the way marked out by God is always the best way, but are you prepared to take the leap and live it?

A Christian Response to Believers and Non-Believers

As you dig into the nature of this topic, you will quickly arrive at a point where the road splits in two, viz. how should we respond to fellow Christians who are poor and then non-Christians that are poor? In this chapter, I kick off by examining Jesus Christ's greatest commandment. The significance of its link with how Christians should respond to the poor will be made clear in the following pages.

Christian Brothers and Sisters

The Greatest Command

The discussion about the "greatest of all commands" (Matthew 22.37-39; Mark 12.30-31), was the scene for yet another test for Jesus. It appears that the Pharisees were satisfied with His answers regarding the resurrection, but now they wanted to test Him concerning the law. They enlisted one of their experts in the law to challenge Jesus with a question, "Teacher, which is the great commandment in the law?" (Matthew 22.36 NKJV). In answer, Jesus replied: "Love the Lord your God with all your heart and with all your soul and with all your mind. This is the first and greatest commandment. And the second is like it: Love your neighbor as yourself. All the Law and the Prophets hang on these two commandments" (Matthew 22.37-40).

This statement essentially is about total obedience to God and service to one's neighbour. The citation originated from Deuteronomy 6.5 (according to Matthew which includes "heart") and this constituted part of the Shema (Deuteronomy 6.4-9; 11.13-21; Numbers 15.36-41), the credo par excellence of Judaism. The fact that the passage refers to heart, soul and understanding (mind) emphasizes the totality of the person involved. One notices from Young's translation that the second command "Thou shalt love thy neighbor as thyself" (Matthew 22.39 YLT) is not second in importance to the first. Both commands are of equal significance. The one is as urgent as the other. The second command is a quote from Leviticus 19.18, where "neighbour" implied "fellow Israelite" or "resident in Israel".[189]

The Metaphor of the Sheep and the Goats

Through the metaphor of the sheep and the goats Jesus emphasizes care for the poor brother or sister. At the second coming and final judgment of God, the "King" (Matthew 25.31) extends an invitation to those on His right hand, the sheep, to enter the kingdom God had prepared since the beginning of creation. What is vital to note is the basis of their entrance is determined by their *actions*, "For I was hungry, and you fed me. I was thirsty, and you gave Me a drink. I was a stranger, and you invited Me into your home. I was naked, and you gave Me clothing. I was sick, and you cared for Me. I was in prison, and you visited Me" (Matthew 25.35-36 NLT).

Those who are invited into the kingdom respond that they do

---

[189]D. Hill. *The New Century Bible Commentary: The Gospel of Matthew*, Grand Rapids, Mich.: Eerdmans Publishing, 1972, pp. 306-307.

not recall ever having ministered directly to the King (Matthew 37-39). However, the King's answer is that they executed these services for the least of these brothers of "Mine," and by so doing were ministering to the King (25.40).

The most popular interpretation of this passage is that Jesus' "brothers" (25.40) relate to Christians because the term *adelphoi* elsewhere in Matthew does not imply that biological siblings are in view (Matthew 5.22-24, 47; Matthew 7.3-5; Matthew 12.48-50; Matthew 18.15, 21, 35; Matthew 23.8; Matthew 28.10). In addition to this, the "little ones", of which "the least" (Matthew 25.40, 45) is the superlative form, also refer, without exception, to disciples in other passages in Matthew (5:19; 10:42; 18:6, 10, 14). Should one accept this, it implies that this section carries similar meaning to Matthew 10:42, "And whoever shall give to drink to one of these little ones a cup of cold water only in the name of a disciple, verily I say to you, he shall by no means lose his reward." (RWB).[190] Jesus' "family" (Christians) must take care of each other in the areas of food, drink, lodging, clothing, health, loneliness etc. The main point is that when the Lord returns, judgment will be forthcoming. One of the criteria for that judgment will be the quality of the relationships that exist between Christians, that quality of relationship encompasses all aspects of life and utilizing them to the fullest (goods included). Jesus clearly placed great importance on taking care of the poor and needy. He states that there will come a time when people failing to do this will be told "Depart from me, you who are cursed, into the eternal fire prepared for the devil and his angels" (Matthew 25.41b NIB).

These passages emphasize the fact that Christians must help

---

[190]C.L. Blomberg. *Neither Poverty nor Riches: A Biblical Theology of Material Possessions* Grand Rapids, Michigan & Cambridge, U.K.: Eerdmans Publishing, 1999, p. 126.

other poor and needy "Christians," but what about the Christians and churches' duty in assisting the secular poor and needy?

The Non-Believer

Thankfully, there are at least a few passages which allude to principles and teachings which require that Christians help the secular poor and needy, namely the "Parable of the Good Samaritan", the "True righteousness being revealed through love" and "The metaphor of inviting the outcast."

The Parable of the Good Samaritan

An expert in the Law asked Jesus, "Teacher, what shall I do to inherit eternal life?" (Luke 10.25b). This question appears to have occurred regularly (see Matthew 19:16-22; Luke 18:18-23; John 3:1-15). Having answered the man's question, Luke records an interesting addition to that mentioned in Matthew 22.36ff., that the man wished to justify himself. "But he, desirous of justifying himself, said to Jesus, *And who is my neighbor?*" (Luke 10:29 DBY – my emphasis). Jesus answered by telling the Parable of the Good Samaritan.

According to the Jews, "neighbour" referred to any other member of the Hebrew race. However, according to Christ, "neighbour" referred to any other person irrespective of race or religion with whom we live or whom we have a chance of meeting.[191] Jesus clearly illustrated the meaning of who our "neighbour" is through the parable of the Good Samaritan. The parable goes to some length to establish exactly who our neighbour is. As it unfolds, we discover that the neighbour is a Samaritan, one who was hated by the Jews and vice versa. Therefore "neighbour" encompasses all

---

[191]J. Strong. *Enhanced Strong's Lexicon* (Greek No. 4139), Woodside Bible Fellowship, 1995 (CDROM Galaxy Software).

those around us.[192] If Jesus stated that we are to love our neighbour and *all* are our neighbours, which means that those "secular poor" in need are included in the sphere of love which needs to be extended. Jesus ends this parable with the imperative: "Go and do likewise" (Luke 10.37c NIV). Show mercy!

The Good Samaritan further illustrates that we should give without expecting anything in return. The Samaritan demonstrates a kind of generosity that has negative economic implications for himself. [193]

True Righteousness being Revealed through Love

In the teaching of true righteousness only being revealed through love (Luke 6:27-38) Jesus presented seven facets He considered to form part of unconditional love. These included:

- Love your enemies (Luke 6.27)
- Do good to those who hate you (Luke 6.27)
- Bless those who curse you (Luke 6.28)
- Pray for those who mistreat you (Luke 6.28)
- Do not retaliate (Luke 6.29a)
- Give freely (Luke 6.29b-30)

---

[192]The following extract was taken from the "Life Application Study Bible" and concerns the Parable of the Good Samaritan. "To the expert in the law, the wounded man was a subject to discuss. To the robbers, the wounded man was someone to use and exploit. To the religious men, the wounded man was a problem to be avoided. To the innkeeper, the wounded man was a customer to serve for a fee. *To the Samaritan, the wounded man was a human being worth being cared for and loved. To Jesus, all of them and all of us were worth dying for* (My emphasis). Jesus used the story of the Good Samaritan to make clear what attitude was acceptable to Him." R.A. Beers (Genesis Ed.) *Life Application Study Bible* (NIV), Grand Rapids, Mich: Zondervan Publishers, 1997, p. 1823.

[193]D.E. Oakman. *Jesus and the Economic Questions of His Day,* Lewiston and Queenston: The Edwin Mellen Press, 1986, p. 164.

- Treat others the way you want to be treated (Luke 6.31).[194]

Persons displaying this form and depth of love evidenced the same characteristics as God, "and you will be children of the Most High, for He Himself is kind to the ungrateful and the wicked" (Luke 6.35 NJB).

The Metaphor of Inviting the Outcast

The metaphor of inviting the outcast (Matthew 25.1-14; Luke 14.12-24) is yet another passage which might include helping the secular poor.

Jesus was invited to eat on the Sabbath at the house of an important Pharisee. Jesus noted how the people jostled for the best seats at the table. This allowed Him to present a teaching, the main point of which was "For everyone who exalts himself will be humbled, and he who humbles himself will be exalted" (Luke 14.11 KJV). But then Jesus proceeded to speak to the host, saying, "Rather, when you hold a banquet, invite the poor, the crippled, the lame, the blind; blessed indeed will you be because of their inability to repay you. For you will be repaid at the resurrection of the righteous" (Luke 14.13-14 NAB). Marshall suggests that this parable does not mean that one must never invite family and friends around for meals and parties; rather, it has been suggested that these metaphors, which appear to be stated as a plain "not X but Y" really mean in Semitic idiom "Not so much X ... as rather Y"[195] Furthermore, it cannot possibly mean that you should invite

---

[194]Consideration: If we, the well off, were in poverty, what would we like those in better circumstances than us to do in aid of helping us? Surely the so called "golden rule" (Matthew 7.12; Luke 6.31) as well as the other broad character traits discussed in Luke would extend to helping the needy? Also note that Jesus was referring to all people here. Jesus stresses the positive and not the negative phraseology Jews used at the time.

[195]I. H. Marshall. *The Gospel of Luke. New International Greek Testament*

the poor and needy just so that, at a later stage, a better reward can be achieved. Both these ideas are against the nature and teachings of Jesus. The main point of this statement is that Christians should be doing all they can to assist those who are desperate and in "need" (whatever that word may encompass). Furthermore, Christians should not expect rewards in this life time, for their reward is in heaven.

The remainder of the New Testament carries little evidence which can be used to further support the fact that those who follow Christ should be helping the secular poor and needy. But this should not rob the above principles of any of their strength. This brings us to the end of Section B, barring one important question, viz. what does true Christian commitment and praxis demand of the Christian today?

For Reflection

1. "To the expert in the law, the wounded man was a *subject to discuss*. To the robbers, the wounded man was someone to *use and exploit*. To the religious men, the wounded man was a *problem to be avoided*. To the innkeeper, the wounded man was a customer to *serve for a fee*. To the Samaritan, the wounded man was a human being worth being *cared for and loved*. To Jesus, all of them and all of us were *worth dying for*." If you were to observe your thoughts and actions, which of these italicized sections would you fit in with?

2. "Rather, when you hold a banquet, invite the poor, the crippled, the lame, the blind; blessed indeed will you be because of their inability to repay you. For you will be repaid at the resurrection of the righteous." Discuss how these verses make

---

Commentary Grand Rapids, Mich: Eerdmans Publishers, 1978, p. 583.

you feel. How about practicing it sometime?

3. Discuss the following statement: If we, the rich, were in dire poverty, what would we like those in better circumstances than us to do in aid of helping us? Discuss your current attitude toward the poor. Are you truly concerned about them?

4. How do the churches and individual Christians in your society treat the poor?

5. What do you do to help the needy?

The Christian's Commitment and Praxis for Today

This may be a very brief chapter, but this is where the "rubber hits the road". If you have read all the previous chapters, you will have amassed quite a lot of knowledge about poverty and the poor from both a humanitarian and biblical perspective. However, what next? How should we live with this knowledge? Hanks has made three useful suggestions;[196]

- *Self Awareness:* Christians should become aware of their own situation in light of God's attitude toward injustice.
- *Awareness of Jesus:* Christians must recognize who Jesus is and what He did to free them.
- *Commitment:* Christians must commit themselves personally to Jesus and follow in His ways.

Peter Davids also sums up this question very aptly:

The Christian lifestyle must be Christo-centric, eschatological, charismatic and communal. [197]

The Biblical lifestyle will of necessity identify itself as being in

---

[196]T. D. Hanks. *For God so loved the Third World,* Maryknoll, New York: Orbis Books, 1983, pp. 114-119.

[197]P.H. Davids. "New Testament foundations for living more simply," in R.J. Sider. *Rich Christians in an Age of Hunger: A Biblical Study,* London, Sydney, Auckland, Toronto: Hodder and Stoughton, 1973, pp. 50-54.

opposition to many of the established values and lifestyle of its culture. It is informed by a different view of reality. The church must safeguard against being co-opted by the world, on the one hand, and surrendering to triumphalism on the other.

- The Christian lifestyle must be *suspicious of wealth*.
- The Biblical lifestyle will be one of *sharing and caring for others*.
- The Biblical lifestyle will always stress *moderation*.

I will leave you with a sobering thought:

Having considered all the evidence provided in this section, no one may claim the name "Christian" and be comfortable in the face of the hunger, poverty, homelessness, insecurity, injustice, oppression and suffering. Christians need to unite and fight these problems guided by the Scriptures and our Lord Jesus Christ.

SECTION C

The Churches
Ministry to the Poor

The Twenty-First Century Churches' Involvement with the Poor

We have already considered the catastrophic situation concerning hunger in the world. In this brief chapter, I will turn my attention to the church and its efforts to alleviate this dire situation. In 2004, I completed my doctoral studies concentrating on a biblical theology of the poor. Part of that process involved developing a research instrument to study a variety of churches located in South Africa, where poverty and the poor are very much in the public eye.

I developed a simple research instrument to assess churches' involvement with the poor. Twenty-two churches were selected. The churches were chosen for the following reasons: They were large in number and more likely to have bigger budgets;[198] or they were well-known and established in the community;[199] and they were representative of different faiths or denominations.

The following details were gathered from each church:

- The number of members
- Their outreach ministries (involvement) with the poor

---

[198]They had potentially more money to use on various ministries for the poor.
[199]They had had the opportunity to become aware of the real needs within their areas or those near by.

Demographics

The total church population represented by the sample equated to 53,960 people.

The Nature of Outreach Ministries to the Poor

The following information can be gleaned from the survey done on the churches regarding the "nature" of their outreach programmes. In total, the 22 churches were involved in 75 individual activities.

Forty-seven percent (35) of the activities involved "giving free handouts"; 15% (11) involved "evangelism" (church planting and spreading the gospel); 29% (22) involved "caring for people" in the following brackets (the poor, orphans, mentally retarded, sick, or the aged); 12% (9) involve "empowering and equipping" people in various ways (sewing, cooking, reading, and school). This information is tabled below:

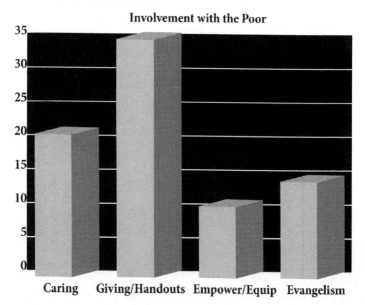

Involvement with the Poor

The majority of churches' main focus was upon giving freely to the poor and needy,[200] viz. clothing, food, Christmas parcels, and monthly collections for the poor.

Conclusions

I would like to begin this section by saying that I recognize the positive contributions and the help these programmes have been to the poor and therefore, do not demean the actions of the churches. There is undoubtedly some equipping and empowering taking place and giving freely certainly has its time and place in terms of response and involvement with the poor, particularly in emergency situations. However, the quandary is that, in the majority of cases, giving free handouts is seen as the only option, and I wonder whether this is the best method of helping the poor and needy? It does not seem to be working. For example, over the last 40 years, the WFP has fed more than one billion of the world's poorest people, delivered over 60 million tonnes of food to 100 countries and committed over US$30 billion for relief and development activities worldwide and the hunger problem still remains dire.[201]

Common definitions of poverty suggest that it is a condition of groups of people we abstractly describe as the "poor," those people with lowness of income.[202] However, the issue is that they are not abstract. People have names, and as was mentioned earlier, they are God's image bearers, and those for whom the ultimate sacrifice was made. The fact is that all people are equally valuable to God.

The world tends to view the poor as a group of helpless people. They become faceless and nameless, and this invites the more

---

[200]Free handouts.

[201] *The World Food Programme - Benetton communication campaign.* 2003.

[202]A. Sen. *Development as Freedom.* (Oxford: Oxford Press, 1999), p. 87.

affluent to treat them as objects of our compassion, people to whom we have the right to act as we believe best. As Christians, in terms of understanding poverty, we must recognize that the poor are people with names, people to whom God provides gifts and people with whom God associates and works – even before we know that they exist.[203] As Dorr states: "To make an option for the poor is not to opt for poverty but to opt for people. It is to commit oneself to acting and living in a way that respects people, especially those who are not treated with respect in our society. It is to proclaim by one's actions that people are more important than the systems that deprive them of their basic rights – the right to eat, the right to work, the right to participate in decision-making, the right to worship according to their conscience, and even the right to life itself."[204]

As was stated earlier, poverty is a complicated multifaceted state which has at its very core the word "lack" in terms of all things essential for material security – particularly in regard to numerous resources leading to physical deprivation.

Myers has some interesting insights which should be added at this point.[205]

It is quite evident that the poor are those who do not have sufficient food, water, housing, schools, infrastructure and other amenities, which generally make life worth living. Therefore, we, the affluent, plan to provide those things which are missing: food

---

[203]B. Myers. What is Poverty Anyway? in R. D. Winter, S. C. Hawthorn (Gen. Ed.). *Perspectives on the world Christian movement. A Reader, Third Ed.* (Pasadena, California: Paternoster Publishing, 1999), p. 578.

[204]D. Dorr. *Spirituality and Justice.* (Dublin: Gill and Macmillan, Maryknoll, New York: Orbis, 1984), p. 77.

[205]B. Myers. What is Poverty Anyway? in R. D. Winter, S. C. Hawthorn (Gen. Ed.). *Perspectives on the world Christian movement. A Reader, Third Ed.* (Pasadena, California: Paternoster Publishing, 1999), pp. 578-579.

aid, low-cost housing, etc. We also identify that many of the poor lack knowledge, for example, they do not understand nutrition, the importance of proper child spacing, how to save money, or run a small business. Consequently, we provide programmes which attempt to educate them. Then we assume that when the poor have the necessary knowledge that they will no longer continue in poverty. Then there is a further ingredient which can be added to the pot: the non-Christian poor do not have knowledge about Jesus Christ and the gospel. Thus, to understand poverty holistically, Christians add the gospel to the "list of things" the poor lack.

These notions about poverty are true and to some degree helpful: the poor do require provisions, knowledge, and the opportunity to hear the good news. Nonetheless, restricting our comprehension of poverty to these parameters presents some serious problems.

For instance, by restricting our understanding of poverty in this way we see ourselves as the providers. This implies that the poor become passive beneficiaries, incomplete human beings which we make whole. This unintentional mind-set has two negative repercussions:

- First, this mindset humiliates and devalues the poor. Our view of them, which promptly translates into their opinion of themselves, is that they are defective and inadequate.
- Second, our way of thinking about ourselves can become messianic. We are enticed into believing that we are the liberators of the poor and that we make their lives complete.

So, in light of what has been said, what possible methods or means might be used to help the poor and needy, besides sharing the Christian gospel? I would like to suggest that whatever these methods or means are, that they not only aim to alleviate hunger, but also aim to ensure a balanced nutritional diet, improve the general quality and quantity of the family, enhance the individual's level of health, restore dignity, self-worth and respect to both the individual and household and improve the relational quality amongst family members.

For Reflection

1. What have you done as an individual, recently, to aid the poor?
2. Consider your church in terms of the following:
    a. What ministry/s does your church have in place to assist the poor?
    b. How does your church stack up with the findings in this chapter, i.e. the churches researched main areas of ministry were focused on giving freely to the poor and needy, viz. clothing, food, Christmas parcels, and monthly collections for them? Are their efforts mainly about 'giving' as mentioned in this question?
    c. Does your church do anything to equip/empower the poor?
    d. What can you do to help your church improve their impact on aiding the poor?
3. What are your thoughts in regard to the proverb: "Give a man a fish; you have fed him for today. Teach a man to fish; and you have fed him for a lifetime?"

Summary

Over the past decade, I have identified certain problems within the context of "Christianity and the Poor," viz.:

- The churches lack of awareness concerning the dire position of the poor worldwide;
- The general lack of biblical knowledge among Christians with respect to God's concern for the poor and our role in assisting them; and
- A concern over the current methods utilized by local churches to minister to the poor.

This book has thus been an endeavour to, 1) provide you and, hopefully through you, your local church, an awareness of some of the facts concerning the dire position of the poor worldwide; 2) equip you with a "substantial" biblical knowledge of the poor, God's concern for them, and His expectations for you and I in regard to them and; 3) open your eyes to the current ways in which local churches typically assist the poor.

More specifically, in Section A, I presented you with a selection of staggering statistics concerning the plight of the poor. I highlighted that the overarching method of "giving freely," which is utilized by local churches, and many relief agencies worldwide, cannot match the ever increasing problem of hunger;[206] we still sit with over 925 million people who are malnourished and 22,000 children under the age of 5 who are dying daily from starvation. Then, I addressed the issue of poverty. I found that trying to establish a definition of poverty is an extremely challenging and controversial task. However, after carefully researching the topic, I identified certain approaches which can be utilized in an attempt to define poverty. They include: the "income approach," "social exclusion," "capability depravation," and "participatory poverty." Following this, I resolved to formulate my own working definition of poverty. I did all of this because I believe that it is important to establish what poverty is in order to develop the best multi-pronged attack against it.

In Section B, I briefly touched on the Nature of the Kingdom of God. That it is not merely about spiritual matters; neither is it to be confined to simply a "social gospel." Rather, Jesus clearly demonstrated that it is a combination of both. It is the event of God's ruling and reigning in all aspects of His created universe. It represents the in-breaking of the future into the present; a glimpse of what the holistically restored Kingdom of God will be after His second coming and the judgement of humankind. Therefore, if we claim to be seeking first the Kingdom of God and His righteousness, we ought to be functioning in both the spiritual and social aspects of its advancement. Following this, undertook to present you with a study on the Biblical concern and response toward the poor. My findings indicated that God established provisions

---

[206]I refer you back to the evidence presented over the last 40 years, viz. the WFP has fed more than one billion of the world's poorest people, delivered over 60 million tonnes of food to 100 countries and committed more than US$30 billion for relief and development activities worldwide and the hunger problem is still dire. The World Food Programme. Benetton communication campaign for 2003.

to safeguard the oppressed, poor, and needy.[207] Furthermore, that the Biblical narrative demonstrated 1) God's concern for the poor, 2) His vindication of the poor, 3) that He demands like concern from His people towards the poor, 4) that He identifies with the poor and, 5) that He sees them as His people. I also highlighted the value of the human being by indicating that he or she is God's image bearer and therefore, deserves the utmost levels of dignity and respect. My conclusion was that the magnitude of the problem requires that Christians should re-evaluate their lifestyles with regard to what they do with their money and how they can meet the crises of the poor. Two further aspects were covered in this section, viz. 1) that Jesus Christ's mission and purpose was specifically targeted at the poor, and 2) that the Christian has a responsibility to help his "neighbour", whom Jesus Christ regarded as anybody (both Christian and non-Christian).

In Section C, I conducted an evaluation to ascertain the 21st century churches' involvement with the poor. I established that a sample group of churches in South Africa, representing over 50,000 Christians, was primarily involved in assisting them using four methods: 1) giving freely, 2) evangelism, 3) caring, and 4) empowering and equipping. Unfortunately, the bulk of the churches focus fell on giving freely. I then highlighted the negative implications of this form of assistance. Lastly, I suggested that alternative methods to simply handing out food must be considered and implemented. These methods should concentrate on alleviating hunger, ensuring a balanced nutritional diet, improving the general quality and quantity of the family, enhancing the individual's level of health, restoring dignity, self-worth and respect to both the individual and household and improving the relational quality among family members.

---

[207]The poor also include the widow, orphan, and sojourner.

In conclusion, I began by indicating that it is my prayer and hope that having worked through the contents of this book, you will be dynamically challenged and motivated to both teach about and do the work of caring for the poor.

The million-dollar question is, "has it stirred you in the manner I had hoped?" Are you prepared to take your place at the coal-face where Christianity meets the poor?

> *No other religious tradition I know of gives such importance to the poor or assigns to them such a significant role. For the Bible does not just merely present the poor as deserving of human concern ... nor does it merely point to the plight of the poor as warning against wastefulness and sloth ... the Bible's main concern is to reveal the theological significance of the poor, the part they have to play in saving history.[208]*

---

[208]G.M. Soares-Prabhu. *Class in the Bible: The Biblical Poor of a Social Class? Interpreting the Bible in the Third World,* (Maryknoll New York: Orbis Books, 1991), p. 153.

Recommendation

My word to the church is that denominational structures and local church boards should urgently and deliberately follow the biblical model of taking a more active role in assisting the non-Christian and Christian poor on a long-term basis. This should be done by educating and training, equipping, empowering and building on-going relationships with those in need.

I would like to conclude with the following verse, which also serves as a challenge to all Christians with regard to poverty and hunger:

> Thou shalt love the Lord thy God with all thy heart, and with all thy soul, and with all thine understanding -- this is a first and great command; and the second is like to it, _Thou shalt love thy neighbor as thyself;_ on these – the two commands – all the law and the prophets do hang.

Matthew 22.37-40 YLT; My emphasis.

APPENDIX 1:
Climate Abnormalities

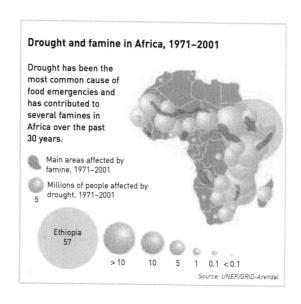

Drought and famine in Africa, 1971–2001

Drought has been the most common cause of food emergencies and has contributed to several famines in Africa over the past 30 years.

Main areas affected by famine, 1971–2001

Millions of people affected by drought, 1971–2001

Ethiopia 57

> 10   10   5   1   0.1   < 0.1

Source: UNEP/GRID-Arendal

APPENDIX 2:
Global Aids Epidemic Summary (2009).[209]

People living with HIV		People newly infected with HIV	AIDS deaths
Adults	30.8 million	2.2 million	1.6 million
Women	15.9 million		
Children under 15 years old	2.5 million	370,000	260,000
Total	33.3 million	2.6 million	1.8 million

[209]Global Report: UNAIDS Report on the Global Aids Epidemic 2010. Geneva Switzerland.

BIBLIOGRAPHY

"The State of Food Insecurity in the World. Monitoring progress towards the World Food Summit and Millennium Development Goals" (Rome, Italy), report of the Food and Agricultural Organization of the United Nations. Reports for 2000, 2003, 2010.

R.A. Beers Genesis Ed. *Life Application Study Bible* NIV. Grand Rapids, Mich: Zondervan Publishers, 1997.

C.L. Blomberg. *Neither Poverty nor Riches: A Biblical Theology of Material Possessions.* Grand Rapids, Michigan and Cambridge, U.K.: Eerdmans Publishing, 1999.

S. Bont-Ankomah. *Addressing food insecurity in South Africa*, Paper presented at the SARPN conference on Land Reform and Poverty Alleviation in Southern Africa Pretoria, June 2001.

H. Botterweck and H. Ringren. *Theological Dictionary of the O.T.,* I–III, 1974ff. VI.

H. Bultema. "Will There Be Recognition in Heaven?" *Bibliotheca Sacra.* Dallas Theological Seminary, Vol. 95:380, October 1938. CDROM Galaxy Software.

B.D. Chilton. "Jesus and the Jubilee," *The Living Pulpit.* Volume 10, no 2 April-June 2001.

L. W. Countryman. *Dirt, Greed, and Sex: Sexual Ethics in the NT and their Implications for Today.* London: IVP, 1989.

Clerical Illusion, Crisis, February 1990.

J. N. Darby. *The Holy Scriptures: A new translation from the original languages.* Oak Harbor: Logos Research Systems. (1996).

P.H. Davids. "New Testament foundations for living more simply," in R.J. Sider. *Rich Christians in an Age of Hunger: A Biblical Study.* London, Sydney, Auckland, Toronto: Hodder and

Stoughton, 1973.

D. Dorr. *Spirituality and Justice,* Dublin: Gill and Macmillan, 1984.

R. de Vaux, *Ancient Israel.* London: Darton, Longman and Todd, 1973.

Economic Rationale for Investing in Micronutrient Programs, A Policy Brief Based on New Analyses, Washington, DC, USAID, 1992.

M. Faber, V. B. Jogessar, & A. J. S. Benadé.. "Nutritional status and dietary intakes of children aged 2-5 years and their caregivers in a rural South African community," *International Journal of Food Sciences and Nutrition,* 2001.

F.C. Fenshaw. "Widow, Orphan and Poor in ancient and near eastern legal and wisdom literature." *Journal of Near Eastern Studies.* 1962 Vol. 21,

J. H. Fish III. "The Commission of Isaiah." *Emmaus Journal,* Volume 4:1, Summer 1995.

"Food insecurity and AIDS: A vicious circle," a report of the Food and Agricultural Organization of the *United Nations* (FAO), 2002.

F. E. Gaebelein E. Gaebelein, R. J. Sider Ed.. *Old Testament Foundations for Living More Simply.* London: Hodder and Stoughton, 1982.

D. F. Gibson. "Applying the New Testament Metaphors. A Case Study: The Alien." *Michigan Theological Journal.* Michigan Theological Seminary. Vol. 1:2 Fall 1990. CDROM Galaxy Software.

The Holy Bible: English standard version. Wheaton: Standard Bible Society. 2001.

The Holy Bible: King James Version. (electronic ed. of the 1769 edition of the 1611 Authorized Version.). Bellingham WA:

Logos Research Systems, Inc. 1995

The Holy Bible: New American Standard Bible: 1977. Foundation Publications. 1997.

The Holy Bible: New American Standard Bible: 1995 update. LaHabra, CA: The Lockman Foundation. 1995.

The Holy Bible: New International Version. (electronic ed.). Grand Rapids: Zondervan. 1996, c1984.

The Holy Bible: New King James Version. Nashville: Thomas Nelson. 1982.

The Holy Bible: New Living Translation. „Text edition"--Spine. (2nd ed.). Wheaton, Ill.: Tyndale House Publishers. 2004.

The Holy Bible: New Jerusalem Bible. Doubleday Religion; 1st Doubleday standard ed edition. 1999.

The Holy Bible: New Revised Standard Version. Nashville: Thomas Nelson Publishers. 1989.

The Holy Bible: Revised Standard Version. Oak Harbor, WA: Logos Research Systems, Inc. 1971.

Global Hunger Fact Sheet, "World Food Programme Facts and Figures," Italy, Rome: World Food Programme, 2003.

Global Report: UNAIDS Report on the Global Aids Epidemic. Geneva Switzerland, 2010.

D. E. Gowan. Wealth and Poverty in the Old Testament. The Case of the Widow, the Orphan, and the Sojourner. Vol. 41 NY: Interpretation, 1987,

G. B. Gray, Isaiah International Critical Commentary. Poole: T&T Clark Publishers, 1995.

R. L. Harris, G. L. Archer & B. K. Waltke. Theological Wordbook of the Old Testament. (TWOT), Chicago: Moody Press, 1999. CDROM Galaxy Software.

T. D. Hanks. For *God so loved the Third World.* Maryknoll, New York: Orbis Books, 1983,

D. Hill. *The New Century Bible Commentary: The Gospel of Matthew.* Grand Rapids, Mich.: Eerdmans Publishing, 1972.

"How the WFP fights the global war on hunger," *World Food Programme,* 2004.

Q. J. Howitt & D. J. Morphew. *The Kingdom, Human Dignity and the Poor: A Biblical Ethic of Social Justice.* Unpublished course offered through The Vineyard Bible Institute. 2006.

N. Hughes. "The State of Food Insecurity in the World. When people live with hunger and fear of starvation." (Rome, Italy) Report of the Food and Agricultural Organization of the United Nations, 2000.

G. Kittel, G. Friedrich, & G.W. Bromiley. *Theological Dictionary of the New Testament. (TDNT).* Translation of: *Theologisches Worterbuch zum Neuen Testament.* W.B. Grand Rapids, Mich: Eerdmans Publications, 1995. CDROM Galaxy Software.

Investing in the future: A United Call to Action on Vitamin and Mineral Deficiencies. Global Report 2009.

C.S. Lewis. *The Weight of Glory.* New York: Macmillan, 1949.

R. Lovelace. *Dynamics of Spiritual Life: An Evangelical Theology of Renewal,* InterVarsity Press, 1979.

C. Majawa. "The Silent Church Amidst the Suffering Africans". *Catholic University of Eastern Africa CUEA Nairobi* – Seminar Paper, May 1989.

I. H. Marshall. *The Gospel of Luke.* Exeter: Paternoster, 1978.

I. H. Marshall. *The Gospel of Luke. New International Greek Testament Commentary.* Grand Rapids, Mich: Eerdmans Publishers, 1978.

P.U. Maynard-Reid. *Poverty and Wealth in James.* Maryknoll NY: Orbis Books, 1987.

W. A. Meeks. *The First Urban Christians: The Social World of the Apostle Paul.* Binghamton, NY: Yale University Press, 1983.

G. Mills. *Poverty to Prosperity. Globalisation, Good Governance and African Recovery,* Johannesburg: The South African Institute of International Affairs and Tafelberg, 2002.

L. P. Moore, Jr. "Prayer in the Pentateuch Part 3." *Bibliotheca Sacra Vol. 99.* Dallas Theological Seminary 393 Jan, 2002. CDROM Galaxy Software.

B. Myers. "What is Poverty Anyway?" in R. D. Winter, S. C. Hawthorn (Gen. Ed.), *Perspectives on the world Christian movement. A Reader,* Third Edition, Pasadena, California: Paternoster Publishing, 1999.

C. Myers. *Binding the Strong Man: A Political Reading of Mark's Story of Jesus.* Maryknoll, NY: Orbis Books, 1988.

K. Nickle. "The Collection: A Study in Paul's Strategy." *SBT* 48. London, 1966.

D.E. Oakman. *Jesus and the Economic Questions of His Day.* Lewiston and Queenston: The Edwin Mellen Press, 1986.

H. Odendal (Ed.). *Christian Handbook,* Cape Town: Christian Network Media, 2002.

J. C. Parrares. *A Poor Man Called Jesus: Reflections on the Gospel of Mark* Trans. R Barr. Maryknoll, NY: Orbis Books, 1986.

R. D. Patterson. "The Widow, the Orphan, and the Poor in the Old Testament and the Extra-Biblical Literature." *Bibliotheca Sacra.* Dallas Theological Seminary, Vol. 130:519 July 1973.

A. Ralphs. *‚Âni und ‚ânâw in den Psalmen,* Theol. Diss. Göttingen 1891-92, Nr. 8 — Leipzig: A. Pries, 1891.

J. C. Ratzinger. Liberation Theology. A „private" document which preceded the *Instruction of Fall,* 1984.

"Rome Declaration of World Food Security," *The World Food Summit* in Rome, Italy, 1996.

C. C. Ryrie. "Perspectives on Social Ethics Part II: Old Testament Perspectives on Social Ethics." *Bibliotheca Sacra.* Dallas

Theological Seminary Volume 134:534 April 1977. CDROM Galaxy Software.

A. Sen. *Development as Freedom,* Oxford: Oxford Press, 1999.

R. J. Sider Editor. *Old Testament Foundations for Living More Simply.* London: Hodder and Stoughton, 1982.

R. J. Sider. *Rich Christians in an Age of Hunger: A Biblical Study.* London, Sydney, Auckland, Toronto: Hodder and Stoughton, 1973.

G. Smith. The Theological Journal Library CD Version 5. *Journal of the Evangelical Theological Society 2002.* Electronic Edition Volume 40:1.

G.M. Soares-Prabhu. *Class in the Bible: The Biblical Poor of a Social Class? Interpreting the Bible in the Third World.* Maryknoll New York: Orbis Books, 1991.

W. Stegemann. *The Gospel and the Poor.* New York: Fortress Press, 1984,

J. Stover, L. Bollinger, R Kerkhoven, G Mutangadura, D & Mukurazita. *The economic impact of AIDS in Zimbabwe,* Washington: The Futures Group International, 1999.

J. Strong. *Enhanced Strong's Lexicon* Greek No. 4139. 1995. Woodside Bible Fellowship. CDROM Galaxy Software.

R.S Sugirtharajah. *Voices from the Margin. Interpreting the Bible in the Third World.* Maryknoll New York: Orbis Books, 1991.

J.E. TamEzekiel *Faith without Works Is Dead. The Scandalous Message of James.* Bloomington: IN, 1989.

G. Theissen. *The Social Setting of Pauline Christianity: Essays on Corinth.* Trans. J. H. Shütz. Philadelphia: Fortress Press, 1982.

"Vitamin and Mineral Deficiency: A Global Damage Assessment Report," UNICEF and "The Micronutrient Initiative," 2003.

H.C. Waetjen. *A Reordering of Power: A Socio-Political Reading of Mark's Gospel.* Minneapolis: Fortress, 1989.

N. Webster. *The Revised Webster Bible.* OLB Download. Timnats-erah, inc. 2005.

C. Westermann, *Isaiah 40-66: A Commentary* Philadelphia: Westminster, 1969.

"World Food Programme Facts and Figures," Italy, Rome: *World Food Programme,* 2003.

R. Young. *Young's literal translation.* Oak Harbor: Logos Research Systems. 1997.

RECOMMENDATIONS

Quinton Howitt has written a very helpful and comprehensive study of poverty. He covers the current phenomena and causes of poverty, its biblical understanding, and especially God's concern for the poor and Christian responsibility to minister to the poor. In all aspects he does a thorough job. I commend this book to leaders in local churches who want to teach on this theme and motivate and implement ministry to the poor.

Alexander Venter

Author of *Doing Church, Doing Reconciliation* and *Doing Healing*

In writing "Christianity and the Poor", Quinton Howitt has, in his inimitable, intellectually rigorous way, filled a hole in the body of Truth. The subject of poverty and faith is huge, the challenge of it even more so, and the range of possible responses to it mystifying when they are not overwhelming. Quinton has covered the topic so comprehensively that the book offers what I often look for in a volume – a "handle" with which to lift this issue and carry it on my journey of faith and leadership. If you want to know what God has to say about poverty and how we may respond to it in love, you will hear an answer here. If you are a pastor or a teacher, you will find this book a wonderful resource for use by groups of students or small groups in a church, with questions for reflection at the end of each chapter. This is an invaluable, quotable and useable resource for anyone who wants to take their faith, and the equipping of the church in an age of poverty, seriously.

Costa Mitchell

National Director

Association of Vineyard Churches, South Africa

This is essentially a brave book. Quinton Howitt presents facts, statistics and current trends that are sobering, to say the least, yet also presents us in the Church with an unavoidable challenge, to pursue her God-given mandate to care for the poor.

John Mumford
National Director
Association of Vineyard Churches, England and Ireland

77176474R00079

Made in the USA
Lexington, KY
22 December 2017